The
ENGLISH
GARDENER'S
GARDEN

Φ

The Gardens

TANIA COMPTON

Foreword

What a miracle it is to live and work in a country where gardens, gardeners and gardening are recognized as a vital contribution to national artistic expression, and what a joy it is to see so many wonderful examples of that expression displayed and described, and given their historical and horticultural context, between the covers of *The English Gardener's Garden*. This book reminds us not to take the art of garden-making for granted, and of the care this little island devotes to its outdoor space.

In this iteration, the second volume following the global overview of *The Gardener's Garden*, published in 2014, the introductory words to that volume by Madison Cox still apply. The gardens in that book range 'from the world-famous to the unknown, the public to the private, the grand to the intimate, the historic to the contemporary...and garden styles from Baroque formality to naturalistic wilderness.' In these pages, however, the gardens are observed through a narrower geographic lens and with less extreme climatic zoning. Northumberland may have more rainfall than north Norfolk, as Cornwall does compared to the Cotswolds, but the vagaries of weather and range of temperate plants that we can grow are reasonably homogeneous. It is the sheer eclecticism of taste and style that is extraordinary.

Gardens are vessels of fantasy and imagination, practicality and precision. These conjured collaborations are fine-tuned in an ever-shifting dance between the creator, the caretaker and the forces of nature. In *The English Gardener's Garden* we discover so many gardens that are not just a dialogue between art and nature but an entire conversation between the spirits of the creators past and present. Thus, there are many places where sensitivity is needed to honour the existing warp and weft, absorbing the past on the one hand while looking firmly forwards on the other. In the Rock Garden at Chatsworth, Joseph Paxton's baton has passed to Tom Stuart-Smith, a stone's throw from Dan Pearson's emotive haiku in the Trout Stream garden. Pearson's interventions among the ruins of Lowther Castle, the restorations at Trentham and Hestercombe – all are gardens that have risen from the ashes of a neglected past to stride with the times. Hatfield is a miracle of continuity, an unbroken chain of exceptional horticulture stretching back to the first Elizabethan age.

In his preface to *A History of British Gardening* (1969), Miles Hadfield wrote, 'The great eighteenth-century Claudian landscape must not squeeze out the garden whose length of lawn is dictated by the clothes-line'. With a similar spirit in mind, this book's pages turn from Stowe and Stourhead to the roadside miracle summoned from shingle at Prospect Cottage and Charlotte Molesworth's creation from cuttings at Balmoral Cottage. From structure that encompasses the loose shawl of a distant panorama to the close corset of clipped hedges, from twentieth-century traditional (the garden of rooms) to twentieth-century modern (the visions of landscape architects), each creation is conceptually and literally an earthly paradise.

Few are the gardens now created as a foretaste of the life to come, but the desire for a sense of paradise in the here and now is as pressing as ever. The gardens by Sarah Price for Maggie's Centre, and Cleve West's Horatio's Garden, are oases for cancer and spinal-injury patients, offering a place to feel the nurturing effects of water, soil, warmth, plants and light. This is a vital connection to the forces of nature, a haven in which to witness the stirring of the seasons, from snowdrops to sunflowers, through solstices and the waxing and waning cycles of the moon; plant growth in our gardens echoes our daily twists and turns as we spin around the sun. In England, it is as though the fashioning of space and plants – gardening – is the cultural expression of our primitive and elemental souls. What we glimpse in the pages of this book is a momentary capture of a day in the life of these miraculous evolving entities. The process of gardening caught in the blink of a camera shutter through the prism of the garden-obsessed English eye. Or, in the case of Great Dixter – that epicentre around which contemporary gardens rotate – the Turkish eye of Fergus Garrett, constantly refining that most quintessentially idiosyncratic of English gardens.

What all these gardens exhibit is a contemporary iteration of the triangulation Tom Stuart-Smith often describes, 'between people, a place and ideas'. Gardens, according to Francis Bacon in his essay 'On Gardens' (1625), are simply 'the purest of human pleasures'.

TOBY MUSGRAVE

The Story of the English Garden

For more than a millennium, the English have been ardent ornamental garden-makers. Down the centuries, certain fashions and features have been introduced from different cultures and adapted, while others are wholly 'home-grown', but one defining characteristic of the English garden has always been a passion for plants.

When exactly the first ornamental garden was made in England is not known, but it is easy to imagine Bronze Age round houses beautified by transplanted native flora. The known story begins during the Roman occupation, with an impressive pleasure garden made c.AD 75 at Fishbourne Palace, near Chichester in West Sussex. The Roman withdrawal in 410 removed the peaceful conditions necessary for ornamental gardens, but missionary zeal brought Christianity in 597. Horticultural skills were preserved within monastic utilitarian gardens, cloister garths, and the enclosed *hortus conclusus* or Mary garden. William the Conqueror's victory in 1066 marked a return to garden-making, but now protected behind castle walls. Norman royals and nobles made ornamental parks and orchards, as well as herbers. The latter had no prescribed layout, and popular features were lawns and flowery meads (sward studded with flowers), arbours and bowers, climber-clad trellis, fountains and pools, turf mazes and seats, and a flowery tapestry in raised beds in combination with fruit trees. Examples were made at Winchester Castle in Hampshire from 1178 by King Henry II (reigned 1154–89) and a century later by Edward I (reigned 1272–1307) at the Palace of Westminster and the Tower of London. As arbiter of western European taste, Edward's would have been among the finest royal gardens in the region.

The fifteenth-century Wars of the Roses brought another hiatus in garden-making, and Henry VII was busy establishing the Tudor *pax*, but his son Henry VIII (reigned 1509–47) developed power-gardening into a distinctly royal pastime. A key purpose of the gardens at the palaces of Westminster, Richmond, Nonsuch and, especially, Hampton Court (see page 104) was to display a blatant and conspicuous statement of Henry's power, kingship and right to rule. With ingredients inherited from the medieval garden, and spurred on by rivalry with France, innovations included the mount, which offered views over a formal garden now 'railed in' by low fences of painted wooden trellis and featuring knots in geometrical patterns, picked out by low hedges. Sundials became fashionable, topiary was rediscovered, and trellis galleries or covered walks connected various parts of the garden. An exclusively royal feature was 'King's Beasts': wooden poles surmounted with carved heraldic devices that underscored the king's power. They are visible on the first picture of an English garden, the bird's-eye perspective of Hampton Court Palace made in 1553 by Anton van den Wyngaerde.

Unlike her father, Elizabeth I (reigned 1558–1603) viewed ostentation as a sign of loyalty and encouraged noblemen to make magnificent gardens in which to entertain her, for example that at Kenilworth Castle (see page 46). Gardens were walled – now for ornament rather than protection – and the new linear architecture was mirrored in the garden, both being united by another introduction, the terrace. The Elizabethan garden was divided up by walks or 'forthrights' into smaller, often square spaces occupied by lawn (a grass plat), mazes and knots. Their patterns became more elaborate, as arbours evolved into stone buildings such as gazebos, and ornamentation – statuary, topiary, sundials, fountains and pools, and the pleached *allée* – became more ornate. In 1588 the first English general gardening book was published, Thomas Hill's *A Most Briefe and Pleasaunte Treatise*.

The Tudor garden had evolved considerably, but by 1603 it was far behind its European counterparts. The Stuart garden amalgamated new ideas from across the Channel into the English Renaissance garden. Under James I (reigned 1603–25), much was taken directly from Italy: axial alignment more closely bonded house and garden and took the garden further in to the landscape; complex hydraulics in the form of highly symbolic fountains and automata were installed; and grottoes, aviaries and menageries added excitement. Moreover, garden-making became more inclusive, a point emphasized by the title of William Lawson's classic *A New Orchard and Garden*, printed together with *The Country House-Wife's Garden* in 1618, one of an increasing number of gardening books.

Many new plants arrived in the early seventeenth century, especially from the American colonies, but it was not until 1637 that the first proper plant-hunting expedition was made, to Virginia by John Tradescant the Younger (1608–62). Under Charles I (reigned 1625–49), Baroque influences came from France, notably the elaborately scrolled *parterre de broderie*, introduced by his queen, Henrietta Maria, and Charles II (reigned 1660–85) remodelled the Hampton Court Palace garden as a miniature Versailles. Dutch Baroque ideas arrived with the accession of William III (reigned 1689–1702) and Mary II (reigned 1689–94), and works by the fashionable designers George London (d.1714) and Henry Wise (1653–1738) included Badminton, Castle Howard, Chatsworth (see page 24), Longleat and Hampton Court Palace. However, by the early eighteenth century the formal geometric gardens had become formulaic, filled with canals and elaborate water features, *parterres de broderie* and *parterres à l'anglaise* (*gazon coupé*, shapes cut out of turf and filled with sand, gravel or coloured earth), walks and wildernesses (*bosquets*).

As formality began to be rejected – Sir William Temple's essay 'Upon the Gardens of Epicurus', published in 1690, was an early call to arms – a combination of factors brought forth the English Landscape Garden. Prime among them were the seventeenth-century landscape paintings of Claude Lorrain and Nicolas Poussin and the notion of 'the genius of the place' formulated by Anthony Ashley-Cooper, 3rd Earl of Shaftsbury, ideas gleaned on the Grand Tour and a rediscovery of Classical literature.

As Nature became increasingly understood, Charles Bridgeman (1690–1738) became the first garden designer to loosen the bonds of formality. Stowe (see page 70), his first major commission from 1713, was concerned with a vastness of scale and the *genius loci*; but his greatest contribution, the ha-ha or sunken hedge, revealed the 'borrowed landscape' and fused the garden with nature beyond. As Bridgeman did, so also did a number of prominent proselytizers, including Joseph Addison, Alexander Pope and Stephen Switzer (also a practitioner), each popularized the new Nature in his own way.

In the 1730s the multi-talented artisan William Kent (1684–1748), who had worked with Bridgeman, emerged as the perfect aspirant to advance the landscape style. Canals became serpentine lakes, lawns were planted with clumps of trees, distant prospects were brought into focus and small buildings symbolized Classical themes. Kent's picturesque landscapes were idealized works of art set within a tamed, sculpted Nature filled with literary and emotional overtones inspired by Italy's romantic past. Notable commissions included Chiswick House and Kew in London, Claremont in Surrey, and Stowe, but Rousham remains the sole unmodified Kentian landscape (see page 66).

After a decade as head gardener at Stowe, in 1751 Lancelot Brown (1716–83) established a practice, in his words, as a 'place-maker'. 'Capability' Brown built on the foundations laid by Bridgeman and Kent, but his landscapes were wholly English in their inspiration and character. Hugely successful, he worked on more than 200 commissions over 30 years, many extending to thousands of acres, including Bowood in Wiltshire, Chatsworth, Croome Park in Worcestershire, Petworth House in West Sussex and, from 1764, his masterpiece, Blenheim Palace (see page 62). Brown's functional compositions, a masterclass in the idea that 'less is more', used four elements predominantly: expansive tracts of grass; trees, variously in shelterbelts, as single specimens and in 'Brownian clumps' set within grass; water, in the form of large, sinuous lakes that interplayed with the sky above; and meticulously sculpted contours. Horace Walpole's words upon hearing of Brown's death perfectly encapsulates his impact: 'Such was the effect of his genius that when he was the happiest man he will be least remembered, so closely did he copy nature that his works will be mistaken.'

In 1788 Humphry Repton (1752–1818) announced that he had become a 'landscape gardener' – a term he invented – and he worked on over 400 commissions over the next three decades, including Blaise Castle in Bristol, Endsleigh (see page 178), Sheringham Hall in Norfolk and Woburn Abbey in Bedfordshire. Despite similarities in raw materials, Brownian and Reptonian landscape styles differed, with Repton seeing his skill as resting in the combination of the beauty of nature with its convenient use. He reintroduced the terrace as a practical adjunct to the house, often balustraded, embellished with an ornate veranda and ornamented with flower beds. He also had a passion for setting rustic buildings within landscape scenes.

By the early 1820s, fashions were changing again, away from imitations of nature towards gardens as clearly discernible works of art. Simultaneously, with an increasingly wide distribution of wealth, suburbs were being built, so that gardening came to the middle classes. Advice to these new gardeners came from John Claudius Loudon (1783–1843), within the 1,200 pages of the *Encyclopaedia of Gardening* (1822) and, from 1826, *The Gardeners' Magazine*, the first periodical for the general gardener. Loudon also devised the Gardenesque style, which he described in 1838 as 'the production of that kind of scenery which is best calculated to display the individual beauty of trees, shrubs, and plants in a state of culture'.

The 1830s saw the advent of seasonal bedding – big, bold, bright mass plantings of tender annuals, often in geometrically shaped beds – and the architect and garden designer Sir Charles Barry (1795–1860) helped to popularize the Italianate garden, for example at Trentham Hall (see page 34). Drawing on history, it was a jumble of formal styles spiced with typical Victorian excess. Also during this decade, the head gardener Joseph Paxton (1803–65) began shaping Chatsworth which, with Biddulph Grange (see page 30), became one of the two most influential High Victorian gardens. Paxton, working within a Brownian landscape, demonstrated that art and nature could coexist, while at Biddulph a series of wonderfully eccentric compartments by James Bateman (1811–97) and Maria Bateman (1812–95), such as 'China', 'Egypt' and 'India', all filled with exotic and rare plants, showed that art and nature could also contrast.

Good taste was not a Victorian virtue, and by the 1860s dissenting voices were being raised against garden excess. In the 1890s the search for a new direction flared up into 'The Battle of Styles'. Horticulturist William Robinson (1838–1935) argued in his influential book *The Wild Garden* (1870) that gardens should be naturalistic – not imitating natural scenery but full of informally arranged hardy plants. His attacks on architects for 'ruining' gardens incensed the architect and garden designer Sir Reginald Blomfield (1856–1942), who advocated a new formal garden, full of refinement and reserve – and architect-designed. Through the written word the pair were fierce adversaries, but in the event the conflict was won by gardener *and* architect. When Gertrude Jekyll (1843–1932) met Edwin Lutyens (1869–1944) in 1889, they discovered they were kindred spirits, and through their partnership invented the Arts and Crafts garden: innovatively geometrical, full of outdoor rooms and elegant features all filled with colour-coordinated planting arrangements, simultaneously profuse and ordered. Most famous of their more than 100 commissions are the Deanery Gardens and Folly Farm (both in Berkshire), Hestercombe (see page 160), Marsh Court in Hampshire, and Jekyll's own home, Munstead Wood (see page 106).

The clouds of World War I obscured the 'gardens of a golden afternoon' made by the Jekyll and Lutyens partnership, as well as the work of other designers and professionals, such as Oliver Hill, Thomas H Mawson, C E Mallows and H A Tipping. England exited the war a debtor nation in profound psychological shock, but one positive of the inter-war years was the more than 4.5 million suburban homes that were built, and the 'Dunroamin' garden, a pastiche of Arts and Crafts-meets-country cottage. Across Europe, Modernism revolutionized art, but Britain was temperamentally unsuited for its upheaval. Sir Geoffrey Jellicoe (1900–96) observed to this writer that his inter-war gardens were 'dead from the neck up – clients didn't want a Modern garden'. Nevertheless, the idealist Christopher Tunnard (1910–79) presented his vision in *Gardens in the Modern Landscape* (1938). It was a cry in the wilderness, but the seed had been sown, and at the Festival of Britain in 1951 the Modern English garden emerged, albeit almost unnoticed. The garden of the Regatta Restaurant by H F Clark (1902–71) and Maria Teresa Parpagliolo Shephard (1903–74), displayed a new, free form employing the irregular use of rock, plantings of sculptural specimens and groundcover, soft-edged water features and Modern sculpture. The style became popular because it was inexpensive and easily attainable, worked well in a small space, and was subsequently branded 'low-maintenance'.

The 1950s and 60s saw significant landscape designs – mostly public, for example at New Towns, Forestry Commission plantations, nuclear power stations and reservoirs – by pioneering landscape architects, notably Brenda Colvin (1897–1981), Dame Sylvia Crowe (1901–97) and Jellicoe. And, as Jekyll fell from fashion, so too did herbaceous plants. Realizing the potential loss, many of these were saved by Margery Fish (1888–1969), who reinvented the cottage garden at East Lambrook Manor (see page 158), and by Alan Bloom at the Bressingham Gardens (see page 36), where he reintroduced the island bed (first seen at Nuneham Courtenay, Oxfordshire in 1771). And in 1969 John Brookes (1933–2018) melded the love of growing plants with al fresco living in his book *The Room Outside*.

The last half-century has brought the significant and positive rise of conservation, both of wildlife and of historic gardens, such creations as Jellicoe's masterful yet overlooked allegorical garden at Sutton Place in Surrey and Derek Jarman's iconic Prospect Cottage (see page 112). Fads have come and gone, for example those for heathers and dwarf conifers, and for decking. There has also been a praiseworthy return to growing organic and heritage variety fruit and vegetables, and the gardening media has discovered more outlets and become ever more influential.

We end where we began, with the English passion for plants. Notable 'plantsperson influencers' have introduced new ideas: Beth Chatto (1923–2018) extolled the beauties of drought-resistant, damp and woodland gardening (see page 84), while Nori (d. 2019) and Sandra Pope advocated exciting ways to use colour; the meadow was popularized by Christopher Lloyd (1921–2006); and Noel Kingsbury and other practitioners have evangelized the New Perennial movement, ornamental grasses, and the natural or wild garden. An emphasis on highly elaborate planting schemes distinguishes English contemporary gardens by such luminary designers as Jinny Blom, Piet Oudolf, Dan Pearson, Charlotte Rowe, Tom Stuart-Smith and Jo Thompson from, for example, those in the United States, with their more innovative use of spatial design and materials. Today the English garden is for the individual: a private place where, free from any fashion dictate, we may express our creativity, grow what we like and make a nurturing haven. The English garden-maker has never been more privileged.

THE ALNWICK GARDEN

Wirtz International

ALNWICK,
NORTHUMBERLAND
21st century
17 hectares / 42 acres

The garden surrounding Alnwick Castle is not without controversy. When the Duchess of Northumberland opened it in 2001, English Heritage accused her of destroying one of Britain's most important historic gardens: an eighteenth-century 'Capability' Brown landscape modified in the nineteenth century with a formal Italianate garden. In fact the garden was a neglected ruin until 1997, when the duchess decided to create her new garden, working closely with the Belgian father-and-son design team of Jacques and Peter Wirtz.

The centrepiece of the first phase was the Grand Cascade. Every minute some 33,000 litres (7,260 gallons) of water tumble down twenty-one weirs made of local stone, and an exuberant fountain show plays every half hour. The visitor climbs steps lined by the sinuous cascade on one side and an arched hornbeam tunnel on the other. Through Venetian gates at the top, the walled Ornamental Garden reveals the Wirtz signature style: a formal green structure with a Belgian-Dutch feel, defined by hornbeam-covered pergolas, yew topiary, and box and beech hedges. The intricate arrangement of small, formal beds filled with roses, perennials and bulbs, the pleached crab apples and paths interspersed with rills fed from a bubbling pool all create an environment that is both tranquil and stimulating.

With a flair for the theatrical, the duchess added one of the largest tree houses in the world in 2004, and a year later she opened the Poison Garden to grow plants such as cannabis and opium poppy as a fun yet educational experience for children. Another children's favourite is the Serpent Garden, with its water sculptures hidden in the coils of a holly-topiary serpent. In spring the Cherry Orchard is breathtaking, with more than 300 great white cherry (*Prunus serrulata* 'Tai Haku') trees underplanted with 600,000 pink tulip 'Mistress'; and in summer the focus moves to the Roots and Shoots vegetable and flower garden and the Rose Garden, with more than 3,000 roses bred by David Austin.

↓ The stunning Grand Cascade – the UK's largest water feature – is controlled by computers from underground pump rooms.

↑ A tunnel of ivy leads to the Poison Garden, full of potentially harmful plants.

↗ *Delphinium* 'Cristella' frames a rill in the Ornamental Garden.

→ A contemporary fountain plays in the Serpent Garden, where the coils of a topiary snake each hold a water feature.

↓ The Cherry Orchard is planted with over 300 cherry trees and underplanted with pink *Tulipa* 'Mistress'.

HOLKER HALL

Lord George Cavendish,
Thomas Mawson, Kim Wilkie

CARK-IN-CARTMEL,
GRANGE-OVER-SANDS,
CUMBRIA
19th, 20th, 21st century
10 hectares / 25 acres (garden);
81 hectares / 200 acres (park)

↓ Evening light falls across a lawn and part of the formal Italianate gardens near the house.

More than 200 years ago, Lord George Cavendish created what he described as a 'contrived natural landscape' at Holker Hall (pronounced Hooker). Today the gardens continue to evolve under the family's stewardship. Holker Hall has many acres of 'natural' parkland, award-winning walks through rhododendrons and azaleas, and woodlands planted with collections of unusual specimens.

More formal gardens lie close to the sixteenth-century house. The designer, Thomas Mawson, was a local landscape architect who understood the climate and the site. Closely trimmed hedges of yew and box add a traditional formality to the design. Many areas are Italianate in style, from the balustraded terrace to the Sunken Garden (once a rose garden, but now with many subtropical plants) to the Cascade, which resembles the Renaissance example at Villa d'Este, in Italy. A new Neptune Cascade was added in the early 1990s.

A labyrinth and wildflower meadow were added in the early 2000s to link the formal gardens with the park and wider landscape. The labyrinth is based on Hindu temple motifs combined with a contemporary version of a Cumbrian stone circle. Twelve monoliths, seats and gravel paths are all made from local slate. It is a place for peaceful reflection.

Change at Holker is a continuous process. In 2014 Kim Wilkie (see page 138) designed the Pagan Grove, reshaping parts of the formal gardens to create a sunken oval amphitheatre. Other features are timeless: the Great Holker Lime tree is more than 400 years old, with a highly sculptural trunk. The Gulf Stream climate allows many choice trees, shrubs and tender perennials to thrive.

Holker Hall combines parkland, woodland, plant collections and formal gardens with typically English topiary, herbaceous perennials and roses. With a great sense of place and history, it is a garden that has developed in ways that are perfectly suited to its site.

↑ Rhododendrons bring splashes of colour to a shady fountain and pool.

↗ The Great Holker Lime was listed in 2002 as one of the fifty great trees of Britain.

→ Two obelisks mark the entrance to the Neptune Cascade.

↓ The labyrinth was designed by Jim Buchanan and Grania Cavendish based on designs from a Hindu temple.

LEVENS HALL

Guillaume Beaumont

KENDAL, CUMBRIA
16th century
4 hectares / 10 acres

Much of the present Levens Hall dates from the first Elizabethan age in the sixteenth-century, but the famous topiary garden was made between 1689 and 1712 for Colonel James Grahme by the French gardener Guillaume Beaumont, who may have worked under the famed garden designer André Le Nôtre in France, and had been Supervisor of the Royal Gardens to King James II in England. Remarkably, the garden retains much of its original form and contains roughly a hundred individual examples of topiary, some now over 9 metres (30 feet) tall.

The garden planted by Beaumont was essentially a Baroque parterre, the pattern defined by low hedges and probably ornamented with small geometrically shaped topiary: cones, cubes, spheres etc. Over time, and as fashions veered away from such rigid formality, the gardens were not remade, but the topiary was allowed to 'grow out'. It is recorded that the by now large specimen box and yew trees were recut around 1815, as formality became fashionable once more. Their forms have gradually evolved into what we see today,

with the original parterre now underplanted with that Victorian staple, bedding plants. Interestingly, during the Victorian period the garden found favour with those championing the Italianate style – basically a hotchpotch of formal features pinched from Renaissance and Baroque gardens, supplemented with plantings of newly introduced exotics; later in the century it was appreciated anew by those espousing the Arts and Crafts garden, with its romantic medieval associations.

But there is more to the garden than just its topiary. Often overlooked is the larger square garden divided into quarters by the Beech Walk. It boasts a bowling green, a fountain garden, fine herbaceous borders, a productive garden, a nuttery, a herb garden, and a romantic old orchard and bee garden. Juxtaposed to it and dating from around 1694, Levens has what is claimed to be the first recorded example of a ha-ha in an English garden. Beyond is the park, also laid out by Beaumont and described by the writer William Gilpin in 1776 as 'a happy combination of everything that is lovely and great in landskip'.

↓ Gardens are an ever-changing artwork, and here what were once small topiaries ornamenting a seventeenth-century Baroque parterre have evolved into the garden's most famous feature.

↑   A dusting of snow emphasises the eclectic and idiosyncratic shapes and forms that grace the topiary garden, offering structural appeal after the summertime underplanting of bright bedding plants has passed.

↑   The gentle, sinuous form of this tightly clipped yew rimed with frost is highly sensual.

↓   The topiary garden is home to over a hundred works cut into abstract and geometric forms. Some even have names, for example the Great Umbrella Tree, the Jug of Morocco Ale, the Judge's Wig, Queen Elizabeth I and her Maids of Honour, and the Toppling Wedding Cake.

LEVENS HALL

LOWTHER CASTLE GARDEN

Sir John Lowther,
Thomas Mawson,
Dan Pearson

PENRITH, CUMBRIA
19th, 21st century
52.6 hectares / 130 acres

↓ Dan Pearson has reconsidered the landscape around Lowther Castle in Cumbria, adding new layers to an existing history. The gardens were originally laid out in the seventeenth century by Sir John Lowther, who employed garden designers such as Thomas Mawson, among others.

Designer Dan Pearson's mesmerizing and imaginative design for the garden at Lowther Castle in Penrith, Cumbria, draws on the romantic archetype of nature's reclamation of a gothic ruin. A twenty-year masterplan, devised by Pearson in 2012, reimagines the garden around the ruins of the castle by adding new layers to an existing history. The planting is masterful, with an abandoned aesthetic and an intuitive sense of its setting.

Inside the crumbling castle walls – the original building dates from between 1806 and 1814 – quasi-wild planting is reminiscent of a lost garden. Climbers, such as flame nasturtium (*Tropaeolum speciosum*) and purple-flowered chocolate vine (*Akebia longeracemosa*) are trained horizontally on the interior walls so that their flowers hang down; at ground level, pools of green *Hakonechloa macra* grass and the ferns *Dryopteris wallichiana* and *D. cycadina* are speckled with bright yellow Welsh poppies in summer.

In front of the main ruin is the parterre, known as the Tapestry Garden. Here nepetas, salvias, thalictrums and sanguisorbas in muted tones are woven with the tall grass *Panicum virgatum* 'Rehbraun' and yew hedging. *Salvia pratensis* 'Indigo', *Stachys byzantina* and *Potentilla nepalensis* 'Miss Wilmott' grow cheek by jowl with *Baptisia australis* and *Actaea* 'James Compton', to painterly effect. The layout of the plants is rhythmic, hinting at an oversized, threadbare needlepoint, their grid-like arrangement and the structural nature of the hedging and grasses suggesting the warp and weft of the fabric.

Further afield is a rose garden where concentric circles of over 2000 roses mimic the unfurling petals of a rose. In a pleasing melding of the original and the new, jets of water from an existing Victorian fountain create the stamens of the flower. Beyond is a wildflower meadow and woodland paths that lead to a moss-covered rockery ruin, a Japanese garden and a sweet-scented garden. There is also a minimalist, contemporary courtyard, harmoniously drawing together the historic and the new.

↑ ↓　Inside the castle, Pearson's planting design heightens the sense of mystery. The original windows offer glimpses of the landscape beyond.

↓　In this detail of the Tapestry Garden, the rhythm and architecture of the plants create a visual link to the castle.

RYDAL HALL

Thomas Mawson,
Sir Daniel le Fleming

RYDAL, CUMBRIA
17th, 19th, 20th century
0.6 hectares / 1.5 acres (terraced
garden); 6 hectares / 15 acres (park)

↓ The circular pool at the heart of the
terraced gardens is aligned on the central
axis of Mawson's garden.

Rydal Hall combines formal terraces with the romantic landscape of the Lake District and the rushing waters of the beck tumbling down the hill. Thomas Mawson, whose family owned a nursery in nearby Windermere, was asked in 1909 to design a garden for the south range of Rydal Hall. His designs were often in the Arts and Crafts vein, favouring a formal structure of garden compartments with expert planting. Whereas Lutyens and Jekyll drew on the local vernacular, Mawson was inspired by the revival of interest in Italian Renaissance gardens. At Rydal Hall he created a series of Italian-inspired terraces linked by twin flights of steps, the lowest of which embraces a semicircular portico.

By the 1950s the terraced gardens had fallen into decay, but they were restored in the mid-2000s and once again feature manicured lawns set with formal flower beds edged with box and planted with a period-correct display. There is ornament in the form of topiaried yew and planted urns on pedestals, pergolas set over benches, herbaceous borders against the terrace walls and fountain jets playing in the circular pool. Mawson used exposed precast concrete for the balustrading, stairs, urns and other features, but it did not weather well, and much has been recast using moulds found in the basement of the house.

Rydal Beck flows to the west of the terraced garden to a waterfall. Beside the pool at its base stands the Grot – now called the Grotto – a little stone building with a window for viewing the waterfall. It was part of a mid-seventeenth-century Picturesque landscape created by Sir Daniel le Fleming and later described by William Wordsworth in his poem 'An Evening Walk'. A secluded area of woodland, with ponds and paths leading to the beck, offers peace and reflection. The Walled Garden has been restored and is again a productive vegetable garden, and scattered through the park is an interesting sculpture collection.

↑ The tall flowers of alliums rise above the verdant, richly planted beds that soften the overall formality of the terraced garden.

↗ A wooden bench in a niche set into the wall of one of the terraces allows the visitor to take in the surrounding planting.

→ Rydal Beck tumbles down a waterfall into a pool beside the Grotto, a small summerhouse built for viewing the falls.

GRESGARTH
HALL GARDENS

Arabella Lennox-Boyd

CATON,
LANCASTER
20th–21st century
4 hectares / 10 acres

Gresgarth Hall occupies an enviable location at the mouth of a wooded valley with the sweeping curve of Artle Beck flowing past the house. However, when Arabella Lennox-Boyd arrived there in 1979, there was no garden to speak of. Over the intervening decades she embraced the *genius loci* and felled woodland around the grey-stone Gothic house to make space for her picturesque, romantic garden; taking full advantage of the valley site, she also opened up vistas and prospects over the borrowed landscape.

The hedges used to ameliorate the effects of the prevailing westerly wind afforded the opportunity to compartmentalize the garden. Today it is a mix of formal and informal, always with the sound of water present. Descending from the house to the lake (in which the building is reflected), the large terraces are planted with clematis and roses augmented by seasonal bedding, the pinks, purples and silver-whites harmonizing with the stone of the house. Complementing this formality near the house are a circular lawn

and richly planted, yew hedge-enclosed double herbaceous borders; the compartment also features pebble mosaics by Maggy Howarth. On the slopes above the beck, planted informally, is the arboretum, a collection of rare and unusual shrubs and trees, including 200 magnolias and the National Collection of the Styracaceae family.

Intimate paths wind through the garden, the meeting points of which are emphasized by 'little theatres': small circles of yew draped with wisteria. The paths variously lead to the functioning kitchen garden, which boasts an elaborate potager; through the Spring Walk, a meadow studded with mostly white-flowered daffodils over which arch specimens of *Prunus serrulata* 'Tai Haku'; down the southwest valley slope to a river-viewing deck on the side of the house; and across the Chinese-style bridge to a display of sculptures, a folly and a Chatsworth-inspired serpentine walk (see page 24). To roam the garden is to enjoy a constant series of delightful contrasts and surprises.

↓   The still waters of the large informal lake, made by damming Artle Beck, mirror the grey-stone Gresgarth Hall and emphasize the shrubby plantings framing the vista.

↑ The misty softness of an autumn morning imbues the rich structure of herbaceous and grassy planting in the wild garden with a delightful pearlescence.

↙ The vegetable garden is both productive and ornamental. Here, structure is given by espaliers, neatly clipped low hedges and low wickerwork, with its rope or barley twist edging; dahlias add splashes of colour.

↓ The architectural formality of the Hall and adjacent top terrace with its stone steps is softened by rich foliage and sculptural flowers: mauve hosta, purple clematis and blue agapanthus.

← Early spring with a backdrop of the delicate pink buds of *Prunus* 'Pink Shell' in the pond borders, a gravel path winds through and is edged by damp-loving plants, such as white marsh marigold (*Caltha palustris* var. *alba*).

↓ Water is a uniting theme in the garden. The naturalistic planting by the cascading steam in the bog garden includes *Gunnera manicata*, lady's mantle (*Alchemilla mollis*) and the native marsh marigold (*Caltha palustris*).

↖ High summer provides a masterclass in how successful and attractive a display using almost exclusively foliage form and tones of green can be.

↑ Mystery and surprise are put to effective use. This small gate by Mark Lennox-Boyd draws one into the vegetable garden.

CHATSWORTH

George London, Henry Wise,
Lancelot 'Capability' Brown,
Joseph Paxton and others

BAKEWELL, DERBYSHIRE
17th–21st century
42.5 hectares / 105 acres

→ The glasshouses of the Conservative Wall contain a remarkable collection of peach and apricot trees, and a camellia.

↘ The setting sun casts a glow over the Great Cascade; steps of different sizes produce different notes of water 'music'.

↓ Chatsworth House with the river Derwent to the west and James Paine's three arch bridge. In the foreground the Ring Pond survives from the seventeenth-century gardens.

In old gardens, it is usual for the new to sweep away the old. That is not the case at Chatsworth, which has a history that stretches from the Baroque garden laid out by the famous seventeenth-century designers George London and Henry Wise to a Sensory Garden opened early in the third millennium.

Vestiges of the first design include the Great Cascade and the Canal Pond, the 1st Duke's greenhouse, the Temple of Flora and the Willow Tree fountain. The outline of the Great Parterre (1699) was revealed during the summer drought of 2022. The greatest legacy of the eighteenth century is the 'Capability' Brown park, emphasizing the natural landscape from near the house.

Chatsworth reached its zenith in the nineteenth century, when the 6th Duke and his head gardener, Joseph Paxton, created one of the two most influential English gardens of the time (with Biddulph Grange; see page 30). Chatsworth's eclectic features showed how art and nature could coexist.

Paxton planted the Arboretum (1835), erected the Great Conservatory (1840) and arranged boulders into a huge rockery (1842; now reworked by Tom Stuart-Smith). Paxton also built the Conservative Wall (c.1832) for growing fruit and camellias, turning it into a series of stepped greenhouses in 1848–50. For a planned visit of Tsar Nicholas of Russia, he installed the Emperor Fountain.

Many of Paxton's features remain in the grounds around the house, but the Great Conservatory and the bespoke glasshouses – including the Water Lily House, where he achieved the first garden flowering of the giant water lily *Victoria amazonica* in 1849 – have all gone. But new features have been added: the Serpentine Hedge (1953); the Maze (1962), with 1,209 yews; a new Kitchen Garden (1980s); and Dan Pearson replanted the original trout stream in 2015–16. Modern sculptures introduce a contemporary feel to the historic garden, helping to bring it into another century of fascinating evolution.

24

← Looking across to the maze and the 'Capability' Brown landscape beyond from Arcadia, a newly developed area of the garden. Planting features perennials and grasses, including aster, geranium, iris, phlox and pulmonaria, as well as rhododendrons, hydrangea and euonymus.

→ The return view up the Hundred Steps to the Arboretum. The steps lead to a monumental contemporary sculpture at the top: *Chaos Meteoro* (2015), by Jedd Novatt.

↓ The maze was designed in 1962 by Denis Fisher for the 11th Duke and required 1,209 yews (*Taxus baccata*). It was made on the site of Joseph Paxton's Great Conservatory (completed in 1840 and removed in 1919).

← The Trout Stream, designed by Dan Pearson, provided the inspiration for the Best Show Garden at the RHS Chelsea Flower Show in 2015. Much of that garden was brought to Chatsworth and integrated along the real Trout Stream, with additional planting in 2016.

↓ *Natural Course* (2020), created by Laura Ellen Bacon of local stone, seems to flow down a woodland slope in Arcadia. The restoration of the gardens, including Arcadia, is being led by Tom Stuart-Smith.

→↘ The rock garden was created from 1842 by Joseph Paxton as a reminder of the 6th Duke's visit to the Alps during his Grand Tour. It reveals Paxton's talent for creating an artistic garden that coexisted with the natural. He used local stone but arranged the boulders 'artistically'. In 2018 Tom Stuart-Smith oversaw its remodelling, with improved access and new perennial plantings.

BIDDULPH GRANGE GARDEN

James Bateman,
Maria Bateman,
Edward William Cooke

BIDDULPH, STOKE-ON-
TRENT, STAFFORDSHIRE
19th century
3 hectares / 8 acres

↓   The yew-lined Dahlia Walk – seen here
from the Shelter House – was laid out by
James Bateman in 1842 and restored in 1988.

In their influence on garden fashion in Victorian Britain, especially on the villa gardens of the new suburbs, two gardens reigned supreme: Chatsworth in Derbyshire (see page 24) and Biddulph Grange. Biddulph was created at a time when the fashion was for the artistic: gardens reflected the visible hand of Man, rather than imitating Nature. If Chatsworth demonstrated how art and nature could coexist, Biddulph Grange was the masterclass in how they could clash.

James Bateman, who inherited both money and land, was a devoted horticulturist with a passion for orchids. His work *The Orchidaceae of Mexico and Guatemala* (1843) is one of the rarest books on botany ever published – and physically the largest. He and his wife, Maria, moved to Biddulph in 1840 and created the garden from 1849 with help from their friend Edward Cooke, a well-known painter. The plantaholic Bateman set out to create a garden in which to display his extensive plant collections from all over the world, grouped geographically or botanically.

In order to achieve this, the garden was designed rather as a horticultural theme park, in a succession of more than a dozen linked compartments, the most famous of which are China, Egypt, Cheshire Cottage, the Glen and the Rhododendron Ground. Each has its own character, features and collection of plants. The visitor is constantly amused and surprised by the brilliantly contrived ways in which the compartments are linked. The design is also deliberately inward-looking. The visitor's attention is focused on the immediate surroundings – especially the plants – rather than being drawn to distant vistas.

Such was the Batemans' passion for garden-making that their money ran out, and in 1861 they were forced to move. The gardens subsequently fell into decay, but they have been faithfully restored since 1988.

↑   The Glen, the work of Edward William Cooke, is an outstanding example of a Victorian rock garden.

↗ →   The Chinese Garden, complete with bridge and pavilion, is entered through an Eastern-inspired stone gateway.

↓   Twin sphinxes guard the entrance to the Egyptian Garden with its pyramid of clipped yew.

BIDDULPH GRANGE GARDEN

TRENTHAM GARDENS

Sir Charles Barry,
Tom Stuart-Smith,
Piet Oudolf, Nigel Dunnett

STOKE-ON-TRENT,
STAFFORDSHIRE
19th, 21st century
3 hectares / 9 acres (garden);
121.5 hectares / 300 acres (park)

↓ The contemporary Italian Garden created by Tom Stuart-Smith on the lower terrace is planted naturalistically with perennials and ornamental grasses.

The story of Trentham is one of beauty, decay, near destruction – and eventual restoration. When he remodelled Trentham Hall in the 1830s for the Duke of Sutherland, Sir Charles Barry – best known as the architect of the Gothic Revival Houses of Parliament in London – used a very different approach that he had devised. Although called Italianate, the garden he created in fact plundered English Tudor, Italian Renaissance, and French and Dutch Baroque styles. On terraces leading down to the informal lake created by 'Capability' Brown in the eighteenth century, Barry laid out formal parterres, with pools and fountains separated by paths and ornamented with statues and topiary.

When the local pottery industry polluted both air and river later in the nineteenth century, the duke moved away. In 1911 much of Trentham Hall was demolished, and the gardens left to decay. Nearly a century later, in 2003–12, they were restored when the estate was redeveloped as a leisure facility. The Italianate terraces, now called the Italian Garden, were restored to Barry's original formality. Tom Stuart-Smith reworked the planting in a contemporary, naturalistic design. The result is a beautiful show in high summer, with drought-tolerant species in hot colours on the upper terrace running to cooler colours and species that prefer moister soil nearer the lake.

Flanking the formal terrace, an informal contrast comes from two new areas designed by Piet Oudolf. The Floral Labyrinth at the garden's entrance is a maze of paths through three beds of tall perennial plantings of strong colours and scents. Juxtaposed with it are the Rivers of Grass, a tapestry of ornamental grasses and perennials. In the wider estate a woodland of 200,000 native oak trees has been planted as a Royal Diamond Jubilee wood. The lakeside walk offers views of the River Trent, wildflower meadows and woodlands, alongside the weir and along nature trails. There is much to explore and be inspired by, including a lakeside naturalistic planting design by Nigel Dunnett.

↑ The upper terrace of the Italian Garden is a traditional, formal arrangement of parterres.

← A gravel path runs through the Floral Labyrinth, designed by Piet Oudolf, with borders of tall perennials and ornamental grasses, including sedum and monarda.

↓ A border designed by Oudolf is filled with *Eupatorium*, *Solidago*, *Helenium*, *Phlox* and *Datisca cannabina*.

THE BRESSINGHAM GARDENS

Alan Bloom,
Adrian Bloom, Robert Bloom

BRESSINGHAM, NORFOLK
20th–21st century
7 hectares / 17 acres

↓ → [pages 38–39] The Dell Garden features the island beds championed by Alan Bloom. Among the plants providing contrasts of colour, texture and shape in a mixed border are evergreen conifers, silver birch, feather reed grass (*Calamagrostis* × *acutiflora* 'Overdam'), eastern redbud (*Cercis canadensis*) and dwarf silver grasses (*Festuca glauca*).

At Bressingham some of Europe's outstanding plant combinations create a vibrant garden with a use of colour that is unparalleled in its floral extravagance. Founded by the late Alan Bloom in 1946, the gardens also contain a celebrated nursery, managed by his son Robert before his death in 1995.

Bloom was one of the most famous British gardeners of his era, and his achievements were acknowledged with an MBE and awards from the Royal Horticultural Society. He was the first to grow herbaceous plants in island beds separated by grass paths but connected by the clever use of colour and texture. His enthusiasm for this style of gardening eventually led to the creation of the Dell Garden, forty-eight beds covering almost 2.4 hectares (6 acres) where the visitor can spend days enjoying their complexity.

The island beds are just one element, however. In 1996 Bloom's son Adrian made a second garden he called Foggy Bottom. It was one of the first – if not the first – to use conifers for colour, mixing some 500 species with colourful heathers and ornamental grasses. It remains a dynamic garden, even though many of the 'dwarf' conifers are now huge.

There are numerous other gardens at Bressingham. The Summer Garden is full of *Miscanthus* spp. and summer-blooming perennials. The Woodland Garden, which has a central feature of giant redwoods (*Sequoiadendron giganteum*) that are now over 24 metres (80 feet) tall, has been planted with North American species.

The sweetest garden is the Fragrant Garden, which mixes plants that have fragrant flowers and foliage. It is well placed next to a picnic area. A dramatic Winter Garden sets early-flowering bulbs against a backdrop of the coloured stems of cut-back shrubs.

↑ The Summer Garden reaches a peak in August, when a riot of colour comes from dozens of species, including varieties of agapanthus, echinacea and *Miscanthus*.

↙↓ Adrian Bloom's Winter Garden retains interest throughout the year, and mixes woody plants with boldly coloured bark, such as silver birch, red-and-orange dogwoods (*Cornus sanguinea* 'Midwinter Fire'), with perennials, grasses and conifers.

THE BRESSINGHAM GARDENS

EAST RUSTON OLD VICARAGE GARDEN

Alan Gray,
Graham Robeson

EAST RUSTON,
NORWICH, NORFOLK
20th–21st century
12.9 hectares / 32 acres

The garden that Alan Gray and Graham Robeson began at East Ruston in 1973 was just a sixteenth of its present size. Constant development has created a varied plot crammed with horticultural treasures and exciting combinations of plants. Key to the garden's survival was the early establishment of shelter belts against the wind. The outer boundaries are Monterey pines (*Pinus radiata*), Italian alder (*Alnus cordata*), Tasmanian snow gum (*Eucalyptus coccifera*) and holm oak (*Quercus ilex*), with inner defences of evergreen shrubs. Hornbeam and beech are used for some internal hedges.

The many pools, hedges, banks and wild areas make the garden a haven for a wide range of mammals, insects and birds. Areas close to the house are more intimate, such as the walled Gravel Garden, while those further off are more expansive, including such areas as the breathtaking meadow, the cornfield, the Desert Wash and the California Garden.

The Desert Wash, designed in 2014, was inspired by an Arizona desertscape. It is filled with drought-loving plants from California, Mexico, South Africa and Australia, and a carefully engineered system drains water away deep below the surface.

Colour in the borders, containers and extensive vegetable garden provides seasonal interest, as does foliage shape and texture. Statuary and borrowed features, such as the Happisburgh lighthouse and the church, offer focal points at the end of long vistas.

Both Gray and Robeson have great plant passions, and both are involved in all aspects of this high-maintenance garden. The most recent areas include the Diamond Jubilee Walled Garden, a Fruit and Vegetable Garden, an orchard of heritage fruit trees, and extensive planting in the East Park. In addition, as the garden matures, choices must be made about cutting back or removing overgrown plantings – hence the decision to build decorative wood piles.

↓   In late summer the Red and Purple Border is bursting with standard ligustrum, dahlias, phormium, hydrangea and fuchsia.

←   The Dutch Garden has geometric box pyramids, balls and hedges around a central *Ilex × altaclerensis* 'Golden King'.

↓   In the Tree Fern Garden *Dicksonia antarctica* is underplanted with maples, narcissi and hellebores.

→   [page 42]   In May the woodland fills with bergenia and delicate forget-me-nots (*Myosotis*).

→   [page 43]   Golden California poppy (*Eschscholzia californica*) self-seeds throughout the Desert Wash Garden, where agapanthus, agave and other succulents thrive.

COTTESBROOKE HALL

Robert Weir Schultz,
Geoffrey Jellicoe,
Dame Sylvia Crowe,
James Alexander-Sinclair,
Angela Collins, Arne Maynard

NORTHAMPTON,
NORTHAMPTONSHIRE
20th–21st century
12 hectares / 30 acres

↓ The borders on Robert Weir Schultz's terrace walk were replanted by James Alexander-Sinclair.

Said to be the pattern for Jane Austen's Mansfield Park, Cottesbrooke Hall is a near-perfect example of Queen Anne architecture, but its gardens are far newer and feature work by many of the twentieth and twenty-first century's finest practitioners. They were begun in the 1930s, when the Scottish architect Robert Weir Schultz was engaged to introduce an Arts and Crafts feel. Part of his legacy is the pergola beneath the ancient cedars of Lebanon, and the long terrace walk with its double borders.

In 1937 the new (and current) owners, the Macdonald-Buchanan family, had Geoffrey Jellicoe add a Renaissance-style balustraded forecourt. Boasting statues and topiaried yew, the box-edged parterre was later softened with herbaceous planting. In the 1950s Sylvia Crowe remodelled the walled Pool Garden, replacing Schultz's rose garden with sunken grass with a circular pool, and trees and shrubs including *Cornus macrophylla*,

Cercidiphyllum japonicum and magnolias. Crowe's arbour offers a vista to the statue of the Gladiator defined by twin avenues of pleached lime (*Tilia × europaea*). Classical statues that once graced the Temple of Ancient Virtue at Stowe (see page 70) now line the Statue Walk, where Arne Maynard has designed informal herbaceous borders with rose domes that appear like topiary.

Several areas had to be replanted after an outbreak of box blight in 2009. In the Philosopher's Garden, the beds are now edged with Lady's mantle (*Alchemilla mollis*). The Secret Garden is today planted with bulbs, hornbeam topiary and oak-leaved hydrangea, while the Dutch Garden was redesigned by Angela Collins as a riot of cornflowers, echium and dahlias. Other highlights include the Herb Garden, with its naturalistic planting, and the Wild Garden, with its wildflowers, rhododendrons, bamboo, gunnera and Japanese maple.

↑　A bridge provides a focal point in the Wild Garden beyond *Darmera peltata* and *Ligularia dentata* 'Desdemona'.

↗　On the Statue Walk, Arne Maynard's broad border contains red dahlias, *Anemone japonica*, *Cleome* and *Macleaya cordata*.

↓　Sylvia Crowe's Pool Garden is a peaceful space with a central pool, a gazebo and a pergola that offers views across the pool and lawn.

KENILWORTH CASTLE & GARDENS
Robert Dudley

KENILWORTH, WARWICKSHIRE
16th century
0.4 hectares / 1 acre

↓ An overview of the restoration in 1990 of the formal yet compact garden Robert Dudley had made to entertain Queen Elizabeth I in 1575. The red structure at the back is an aviary that would have contained a collection of exotic birds.

In 1563 Queen Elizabeth I granted Kenilworth Castle to her favourite, Robert Dudley, 1st Earl of Leicester, who created a new garden fit for his queen's visit between 9 and 27 July 1575. Over the centuries the garden was lost, to be re-created in 2009 based on archaeological excavations of the original garden and the description of it, possibly by Robert Langham, keeper of the privy council chamber, describing the queen's visit to Kenilworth.

The 'goodly garden' is a sunken rectangle, its formal layout geometric; it displays mirror symmetry along both cross-axes. At the centre is 'placed a very fair fountain' that 'cast' its water into 'an eight-square' octagonal basin. Surrounding the fountain and enclosed by low diamond trellis fences of chestnut wood are four rectangular compartments, each containing a pair of square knot gardens. Between them stands an obelisk, originally 'of one whole piece; hewn out of hard porphyry',

but today of wood painted to look like that reddish-purple stone. The beds are raised and enclosed by planks, and the paths, now gravel, were originally of sand: 'not light, or too soft, or soily by dust, but smooth and firm, pleasant to walk on, as a sea-shore when the water is availed'. Each knot is richly planted: 'the sweetness of savour on all sides, made so respirate from the redolent plants and fragrant herbs and flowers, in form, colour and quantity so deliciously variant'. A dominant feature aligned on the shorter axis is the aviary.

The restoration has some inaccuracies. For example, the strips of lawn fringing the rectangular spaces are historically incorrect, and certain elements are out of scale. Nonetheless, it is a splendid re-creation of a Tudor garden lost for almost 400 years. It has been criticized for lacking a certain grace and elegance, but its importance lies in its marking the transition from charming medieval herber to Renaissance grandeur.

↑   The geometrically laid out garden features eight knot gardens filled with plants available at the time the garden was originally made, including strawberries, pinks and sweet williams.

→   The ornate wooden kiosk would have provided the queen with a fair prospect over the garden, which also contained trees bearing her favourite fruit: cherries.

↓   Plants in the knot gardens, include thrift (*Armeria maritima*), gillyflower (*Dianthus caryophyllus*), eglantine or sweet briar and damask roses (*Rosa rubiginosa* and *R. × damascena*). Fruit trees include the apple 'Court Pendu Plat' and the pear 'Black Worcester', both of which may date to Roman times.

THE LASKETT GARDENS

Sir Roy Strong,
Julia Trevelyan Oman

MUCH BIRCH,
HEREFORDSHIRE
20th century
1.5 hectares / 4 acres

This is among the most important formal gardens of the last fifty years, but it provokes mixed responses: some visitors love it; others are not impressed. Perhaps this reflects the personality of Sir Roy Strong, the garden's co-creator, who held strong opinions about which historical garden styles are a suitable inspiration – and which are not. He abhored the naturalism of 'Capability' Brown but rejoiced in the formal gardens of the Italian Renaissance, English gardens of the Tudor and Stuart eras, and gardens created in England before World War I, such as Hidcote Manor (see page 50). Their influence is clear at The Laskett Gardens (which Strong gifted to the charity Perennial in 2020), not only in the extensive use of topiary, building, statuary and ornamentation, but also in the strong architecture. The gardens are laid out in a series of twenty or so 'rooms', including a rose garden, a knot garden, a kitchen garden, and the Colonnade Court. The aim is to thrill, and to offer dramatic vistas.

The very individual gardens were begun in 1973 by Strong and his wife, Julia Trevelyan Oman, and a number of features recall the couple's friends and jobs. An armillary sphere from the garden of Strong's friend Sir Cecil Beaton graces the Jubilee Garden; an arbour honours the choreographer Sir Frederick Ashton, two of whose most famous ballets Trevelyan Oman designed; the Victoria and Albert Museum Temple testifies to Strong's directorship of that institution.

After thirty years Strong decided the infrastructure was over-mature, so the hedges were recut, the planting reconditioned and views of the landscape opened up. The design is not without its critics, but the gardens were still evolving under Strong's direction (Trevelyan Oman died in 2003) until he passed ownership to Perennial. They are a lesson in how garden history can be brought up to date to create a place that owes its inspiration to the past but is also part of its own zeitgeist.

↓ An armillary sphere from the garden of the society photographer Cecil Beaton stands in the Silver Jubilee Garden. In the background is the Triumphant Arch of the Rose Garden.

↑ In the heart of the Kitchen Garden stands a modern copy of an eighteenth-century statue of a gardener.

→ A platform in the Howdah Garden provides views across the site.

↓ An urn in the Christmas Orchard, first planted in 1974, holds the ashes of Julia Trevelyan Oman and will eventually hold those of Sir Roy Strong.

↘ The arms of Edward I, a fragment from the medieval Palace of Westminster, is displayed in the Christmas Orchard.

HIDCOTE MANOR

Lawrence Johnston

HIDCOTE BARTRIM,
GLOUCESTERSHIRE
20th century
4 hectares / 10 acres

Hidcote Manor, one of the twentieth century's most iconic and influential English gardens, was created by an American. Lawrence Johnston, a naturalized British citizen, began his masterpiece in 1907 when his mother bought him a house with views of the Gloucestershire countryside. Over forty-one years he created one of Britain's most visited gardens.

A keen plantsman, Johnston was influenced by the Arts and Crafts gardens of Gertrude Jekyll and Edwin Lutyens in his colour-coordinated planting and use of compartments. He used the sloping site skilfully to create a seemingly haphazard yet rewarding succession of rooms that create an atmosphere of mystery and surprise – albeit lacking Lutyens' finesse.

The scheme uses two perpendicular axes aligned as a 'T', around which are grouped twenty garden 'rooms' – among them the Stilt Garden, the Bathing Pool Garden and Mrs Winthrop's Garden (named for Johnston's

mother) – divided by mixed hedges of holly, hornbeam, yew, beech and lime. But his triumph was the twin Red Borders: the reds of the flowers and foliage draw the eye and bring the foreground into sharp focus, while in the middle distance gazebos frame the contrasting green of the Stilt Garden.

The character of the rooms comes from Johnston's artful planting, a skill he developed in the 1920s with help from his friend Norah Lindsay. The writer and gardener Vita Sackville-West described it as 'a kind of haphazard luxuriance'. Hidcote is unjustly less famous than Sissinghurst, and the characters of the two gardens' respective creators could not have been less alike. Sackville-West was vivacious, stylish and charming; Johnston was described by the plant-hunter George Forrest as 'a right good old Spinster spoilt by being born male'. Johnston's own plant-hunting led him to discover two new mahonias (*Berberis oiwakensis* and *B. napaulensis*), and in his garden he bred *Hypericum* 'Hidcote'.

↓ Morning sun illuminates canna and dahlias in the Red Borders leading past the Pavilions to the Stilt Garden.

→ Tulips in the Old Garden in May make a cheerful contrast to the honey-coloured stone of the Cotswold house.

HIDCOTE MANOR

←   In the Bathing Pool Garden a cherub fountain stands before bird topiary.

↓   *Crambe cordifolia*, lupins and foxgloves flourish in the Long Borders in June.

←   The Rock Bank is home to a Corsican pine and Mediterranean perennials.

→   The planting of Mrs Winthrop's Garden includes *Alchemilla mollis* and bronze cordylines in ornamental urns.

HIGHGROVE

Lady Salisbury, Rosemary Verey,
Isabel and Julian Bannerman, and others

TETBURY,
GLOUCESTERSHIRE
20th–21st century
6 hectares / 15 acres

↓ The Sundial Garden was originally
designed by Lady Salisbury as a rose garden.

Royalty has given the world a rich garden legacy. At Highgrove, King Charles III continues this while demonstrating his belief that it is better to work with than against nature. Highgrove is not a grand landscape garden but the creation of a keen gardener with organic principles. King Charles has been advised by key British gardeners, from Rosemary Verey, Lady Salisbury and Miriam Rothschild to Isabel and Julian Bannerman.

The gardens are mainly informal, but a formal axis from the Georgian house has been created by a path planted with thyme, which in summer buzzes with bees. Alongside the path are yew spheres in fantastical shapes, while the design is delineated by pleached limes (*Tilia*) forming aerial rectangles of green. Beyond is a water feature, and the line continues into the wildflower meadows as a lime avenue ending in a dovecote.

The meadows are the epitome of summer, with a rich matrix of native wildflowers including ox-eye daisy (*Leucanthemum vulgare*), the semi-parasitic yellow rattle (*Rhinanthus minor*) and more exotic species, such as camassia and ornamental onions (*Allium*). The last are examples of the preference for blue and purple in the garden.

In contrast to the open meadows is the Woodland Garden, complete with a stumpery that is home to many ferns. Among the trees are classical temples and a fairytale tree house. *Acer* cultivars are used for their rich autumn colour, as is the purple *Hydrangea aspera* Villosa Group. The Walled Garden is home to a wealth of organic fruit and vegetables.

The Woodland Garden blends into a small arboretum that holds part of the Plant Heritage collection of beech (*Fagus*) trees, echoing the King's commitment to conservation. The gardens at Highgrove are thus a testimony to one man's passion to live and garden sustainably with nature.

← May blooms in the Cottage Garden designed by King Charles and the late Rosemary Verey.

↓ The Kitchen Garden includes rare and endangered varieties that are vital in terms of biodiversity.

← *Camassia*, buttercups and dandelions bloom in the Wildflower Meadow Garden in front of the house.

→ In spring, daffodils welcome visitors to the thatched tree house 'Hollyrood House', in the Stumpery of the Woodland Garden, designed by Isabel and Julian Bannerman.

↓ Golden yew topiary adorns the Thyme Walk between hornbeam stilt hedges.

SEZINCOTE

Thomas Daniell,
Graham Stuart Thomas, Lady Kleinwort

MORETON-IN-MARSH,
GLOUCESTERSHIRE
19th, 20th century
2 hectares / 5 acres

The surprise that is Sezincote (SEE-zin-cote, 'the place of the oaks') is revealed at the final curve of the drive: an exotic-looking house that transports visitors to the foothills of the Himalayas in northern India. A wooded Cotswold hillside makes an appropriate backdrop to this small mansion in the Hindu–Mughal style, built around 1805 by the architect Samuel Pepys Cockerell for his brother Sir Charles Cockerell, an East India Company veteran who wanted a home to remind him of South Asia.

To carry the style into the garden and the landscape beyond, Sir Charles employed the artist Thomas Daniell, who had himself spent a decade in India. Daniell is credited with conceiving the Thornery and the Water Garden, both north of the house; but in reality, the gardens were probably more of a collaboration between client and patron. Sir Charles was involved in all aspects, down to the placement of the Brahmin bulls on Daniell's Indian Bridge. Humphry Repton was also consulted, and the parkland at Sezincote has a Reptonian feel.

A temple to the Hindu sun god marks the start of the Water Garden at the top of the small valley, and the formal pool to the front continues the Indian style. From there, a stream flows along the valley, under the Indian Bridge to the Snake Pool, with its bronze serpent wrapped around a column, ending downstream in two more naturalistic pools. The area was planted for year-round interest by the renowned plantsman Graham Stuart Thomas, who helped former owners Sir Cyril and Lady Kleinwort restore the run-down gardens from 1945 onwards.

Lady Kleinwort added the South Garden in 1965 after a visit to India. The design follows that of a traditional Islamic paradise garden, or *chahar bagh*, with four parts divided by paths or water that represent the four rivers of life. At Sezincote, two canals are crossed by paths of the same dimensions, with an octagonal pool and fountain as a focal point. Along each axis, Irish yews (*Taxus baccata* 'Fastigiata') are used in place of traditional cypresses, which are not reliably hardy in the Cotswold climate.

↓ A temple to the Hindu sun god Surya overlooks the Oriental Fountain Pool.

→ Two elephants stand sentinel over the formal canals of the South Garden in front of the Mughal-inspired house.

↓ Two Brahmin bull statues adorn Daniell's stone Indian Bridge above the stream and Snake Pool.

↘ Ferns and *Lysichiton americanus*, the skunk cabbage, emerge each spring at the damp margins of the Stream Garden, along with other moisture-loving plants.

UPTON WOLD

Brenda Colvin,
Hal Moggridge

MORETON-IN-MARSH,
GLOUCESTERSHIRE
20th–21st century
5.6 hectares / 14 acres

When Mr and Mrs Ian Bond bought the old manor house at Upton Wold in 1973, there was no garden, just two yew trees, a holly and some old apple trees. Since then, helped by garden architects Brenda Colvin and Hal Moggridge, the Bonds have created an original and intriguing garden.

Approaching the house down the long woodland drive, the visitor has no inkling of what awaits. But dart through a path in the yew hedge and stand on the terrace, and you are facing east over a fine garden and a wide valley. The central axis leads the eye down into the valley and up over the woods and fields beyond. The axial Broad Walk is bordered by two massive yew hedges, with windows (*clairvoyées*) cut to offer glimpses of a colourful herbaceous border, and a long iris walk. A dark tunnel runs through the centre of the right-hand hedge – a child's wild delight. Up a bank is the Secret Garden, with magnolias and a fine *Davidia involucrata*, underplanted with bulbs.

Elsewhere are a pond with bog plants, and a wildflower meadow. A large kitchen garden has fruit, vegetables and flowers arranged each side of a path lined with pleached hornbeam; clipped cones of holly, box hedges and espaliered apples and pears are underplanted with hellebores. Stone pillars at the end of the Hornbeam Path lead into the Woodland Garden, with a shelter belt beyond, and a sundial designed by Mark Lennox-Boyd; a cheetah sculpted by Dylan Lewis slinks out of the bushes. A small orchard, canal garden (the canal, fountains and weeping mulberry trees were added in 1995 by Anthony Archer-Wills) and dovecote garden add to the charm of the place.

The arboretum is home to the National Collection of *Juglans* (walnuts) and *Pterocarya* (Caucasian wingnut). Mown paths lead to a focal point formed by a labyrinth, and a circle of twelve standing stones represent the Apostles – and provide a suitable place to stand and contemplate the delights of this garden. The labyrinth was completed in 2013 and leads to the medieval village of Upton, which was abandoned after the Black Death in the fourteenth century.

↓ The Emily Young Border is named after the leading British sculptor whose work provides its focus.

↑   The Canal Garden, which sits on a plateau beneath the house, was created by Anthony Archer-Wills.

↓   Catmint (*Nepeta* 'Six Hills Giant') flowers along the path of the walled Upper Vegetable Garden.

→   Weathered stone balls punctuate the strict formation of a row of Hidcote-inspired hornbeam trunks.

BLENHEIM PALACE

Lancelot 'Capability' Brown,
Achille Duchêne

WOODSTOCK,
OXFORDSHIRE
18th, 20th, 21st century
809 hectares / 2,000 acres

↓ Although much of Sir John Vanbrugh's bridge is now underwater, thanks to the damming of the river to create the lake, it still fits perfectly into the vista towards the palace.

Lancelot 'Capability' Brown marked the zenith of the eighteenth-century English landscape garden tradition, and Blenheim is his masterpiece. But such was Brown's genius that his fingerprints are subtle. He called his work 'place-making', and aimed to create an entirely natural appearance. The politician Horace Walpole wrote: 'So closely did he copy nature that his works will be mistaken.'

Brown did not invent the English landscape garden. Charles Bridgeman first broke the chains of the Baroque formal garden, and he was followed by William Kent's picturesque compositions. But Brown took the naturalistic style to its logical conclusion. He conceived the 809-hectare (2,000 acre) park as a whole, and transformed it into a naturalistic landscape that retained many of the essential features of the earlier designs but united them into a single composition. He created landscapes that were purely English in their character, and which themselves became an inspiration for poets and painters such as J M W Turner and John Constable.

Brown started working at Blenheim for the 4th Duke of Marlborough in 1764, the same year he was appointed Royal Gardener to King George III. Sweeping away the formal gardens behind the palace, he sowed grass and dug a ha-ha to introduce views of the 'borrowed landscape'. Elsewhere he sculpted contours, sowed grass and planted trees – singly, in 'Brownian clumps' and as plantations – in order to control and manipulate vistas. He designed a landscape that begins at the door and disappears into the distance. His masterstroke was to dam the river to create the sinuous lake. It provides a perfect foil to Sir John Vanbrugh's celebrated bridge, although 10 metres (30 feet) of the structure are now underwater. Brown's cascade at the lake's terminus has been restored, and the Queen's Pool (part of the lake) was dredged in 2022. The silt was moved to the Great Park, where a 16-hectare (40 acre) landform (mound) will be created. This land will then be returned to grassland.

In the 1920s the 9th Duke reinstated a hint of formality to provide a transition between architecture and landscape. Both the Italian Garden and the French Baroque-inspired Water Terraces were designed by the French landscape architect Achille Duchêne.

↑   The box and yew hedges in the Italian Garden, created in the early twentieth century, are trimmed precisely using spirit levels.

↗   The Water Terraces are a twentieth-century echo of the great formal water gardens of the Baroque era, such as that at Versailles.

→   An aerial view looking south shows 'Capability' Brown's famed lake in the foreground and the designed landscape beyond the palace.

PETTIFERS

Gina Price

WARDINGTON, NEAR
BANBURY, OXFORDSHIRE
20th–21st century
0.6 hectares / 1.5 acres

↓ ↘ Seasonal views of the Parterre Garden
demonstrate year-round interest. In autumn,
deep-green topiary contrasts with the golden
foliage of Himalayan birch (*Betula utilis* var.
jacquemontii) and yellow *Helianthus* 'Lemon
Queen'. In spring, *Allium* 'Purple Sensation'
contrasts with the linear box hedge and
yew pillars.

Gina and James Price moved to Pettifers in 1984, since when Gina – who until that time had never made a garden – has created a gem that is at once peaceful and stimulating. The garden is an elongated rectangle that descends in levels along a gentle slope towards a medieval landscape and incorporates a 'borrowed' prospect out over hedged fields. Its four main areas are the flower garden, juxtaposed to the house, that leads to a long lawn flanked by deep borders. The lawn transitions via a flight of steps into a meadow through which is cut a sinuous grass path that leads to the parterre garden – a pair of squares enclosed by low box hedges, featuring yew and box topiary. In this lower area are also the Autumn Border and the luscious Klimt Border. At the far end of the parterre is an area of sward ornamented by an *allée* of cut-leaf crab apples (*Malus transitoria*) that are smothered in blossom in late spring.

The geometry of the somewhat awkwardly shaped plot (defined as it is by adjacent properties) is softened and enlivened by rich plantings in the Arts and Crafts tradition. Initially inspired and advised by Diany Binny, an important figure in the development of the garden at Kiftsgate, Gloucestershire from the mid-1950s, Price began her own creative journey, the manifestation of which is seen in the characteristic very wide borders and large drifts of herbaceous plants and grasses, carefully chosen and arranged to ensure the garden offers year-round interest. The result is a very personal, elegant haven, and a true plantswoman's garden.

And, while careful thought is evident in the wonderful planting combinations and arrangement, the very fact that Price has never composed a planting plan speaks of a delightful impulse and experimentation. As she explains, 'I take a couple of things that look good together and work around them.'

← The Klimt Border in the golden light of an early spring morning. The fresh green of the *Cornus controversa* 'Variegata' contrasts with the pale apricot of newly opened *Tulipa* 'Sanne'.

↓ Deep borders contain the grass-like foliage and pink flowers of *Dianthus carthusianorum*; the spiky *Eryngium* 'Picos Blue'; the salmon-orange of *Kniphofia* 'Timothy'; and the contrasting softness of the grass *Nassella tenuissima* (formerly *Stipa tenuissima*).

ROUSHAM HOUSE

William Kent

STEEPLE ASTON,
OXFORDSHIRE
18th century
12.1 hectares / 30 acres

Rousham is a surpassing expression of Britain's confidence during the eighteenth century, when military prowess was enlarging its empire. Fittingly for a garden made for two soldiers involved in this process – Colonel James Dormer, followed by his brother General Robert Dormer – Rousham recalls the glories of ancient Rome and its empire.

At Rousham, as elsewhere, the work of Charles Bridgeman (the pioneer of the English landscape movement) is overlaid by that of his successor William Kent. Only the Long Walk remains of Bridgeman's design, since Kent swept away formality in order to evoke an emotional response to nature. Between 1737 and 1741 Kent created a picturesque landscape – specifically one that evoked the paintings of Claude Lorrain and Nicolas Poussin, rich in classical, allegorical and poetical ideas. At the terminus of the lawn behind the house and at the top of the slope down to the river is a statue of a lion

mauling a horse – an allegory of the British fighting the Spanish. Close by, a gladiator dies in restrained agony, and in a distant field is an 'eye-catcher', an ornamented barn placed to enhance the view. The visitor who enters the understorey of evergreen laurel in the woodland and follows the serpentine walks experiences a Stygian gloom and melancholy but is surprised by hidden statuary and a temple in a glade. Water flows along a sinuous rill in the middle of the path to the Cold Bath. Under the open sky again, one reaches the Venus Vale, with its statues and a pair of (now dry) cascades. Across the sloping lawn is the Pyramid House, built to provide views over the borrowed landscape.

Although the landscape is the highlight of Rousham, the walled kitchen garden is now of great interest, home to herbaceous borders and espaliered apple trees. Elsewhere are a small knot garden planted with roses, and a pigeon house.

↓ The Praeneste contains seats designed by William Kent, with views over the Cherwell.

→ At the end of the lawn behind the house, a statue of a horse being attacked by a lion stands at the top of the slope above the river. In a distant field is an 'eye catcher', a barn placed to enhance the view.

↓ Like the other features, Kent's cascades in the Venus Vale were made from local stone rather than classical marble.

← ↓　William Kent's Temple of Echo (below) and a statue of Apollo viewed along the Long Walk (left) are typical of the classical references hidden throughout the garden.

↖ ↑　A rill snakes along the centre of a path to feed the Octagon Pond, which is overlooked by a statue of Pan.

STOWE

Charles Bridgeman, Sir John Vanbrugh,
William Kent, Lancelot 'Capability' Brown

STOWE, BUCKINGHAMSHIRE
18th century
101.2 hectares / 250 acres

Stowe defines the eighteenth-century English landscape garden. What the modern visitor sees at Stowe is a hybrid of the key designers who developed this highly influential garden style: Sir John Vanbrugh, Charles Bridgeman, William Kent and Lancelot 'Capability' Brown.

Funded by Richard Temple, later Lord Cobham, Vanbrugh and Kent worked at Stowe before Vanbrugh's death in 1726. Bridgeman and Kent then created a Baroque-inspired garden with innovative features, such as the sunken fence or ha-ha, still in use. After Bridgeman's death in 1738, Kent made the garden less formal; he also erected many of its forty temples and monuments and created the allegorical programme that underlines it. The visitor is asked to repeat the Choice of Hercules by choosing between two gardens. The Eastern Garden stands for a severe but glorious life of virtue, where Cobham pins his political colours to the mast in the Temple of British Worthies.

The Western Garden represents a pleasurable but useless life of vice, symbolized by Kent's Temple of Venus, which had erotic murals and a 'pleasuring sofa'. From 1741 Kent worked closely with a new head gardener – then just plain Lancelot Brown – who cut his landscaping teeth at Stowe.

Stowe was the first British garden to have its own guidebook, and in the mid-eighteenth-century visitors arrived from across Europe, popularizing the English landscape garden. But Stowe's role came at a cost, eventually bankrupting Cobham's family.

Today, to walk among Stowe's moulded contours, classical temples, sinuous lake, stately trees and views is to enjoy the best of designed nature. Being able to 'read' the garden makes the landscape that much richer. In 2015 the National Trust, which owns the garden, began extensive restorations, projected to open up a third of the area previously not open to the public.

↓   The view across the Octagon Lake
rises to the Corinthian Arch, built in 1765.

← The sunken stone ha-ha (one of Bridgeman's original features) was intended to keep animals out of the garden without obstructing the sweeping views.

Kent designed the Temple of Ancient Virtue as a memorial to Greek thinkers.

→ [pages 72–73] The Temple of British Worthies is home to busts of Cobham's heroes and heroines.

↑ The Temple of Venus (1731), seen here across the Eleven-Acre Lake, was the first garden building designed by William Kent.

→ The Palladian Bridge was designed with gentle slopes for horse-drawn carriages.

STOWE

TURN END

Peter Aldington,
Margaret Aldington

TOWNSIDE, HADDENHAM,
BUCKINGHAMSHIRE
20th–21st century
0.2 hectares / 0.6 acre

↓ Peter Aldington has used a wide range of plants in a relatively small area, but the results are coherent and every different variety adds to the whole.

Turn End feels much larger than it is, so successfully has it been designed and so much more expansive are its ideas than its size. The garden was created by the architect Peter Aldington as an extension to three houses he built in the mid-1960s to show how dwellings built from modern materials could be assimilated into a traditional English village. Although he intended his family to live in one of the houses for only a short time, they still live there now, and the garden has meanwhile become internationally renowned as an example of a well-designed outdoor space.

Although the house fits into its English surroundings, parts of the garden feel more southern European. The large courtyard is divided into different areas, each with its own flavour or style. A strong grid of sightlines and focal points divides the space so that visitors circulate as their eyes and feet are drawn towards large pots or specimen trees. Hedges delineate spaces,

while walls extending from buildings create smaller courtyards and outdoor rooms.

The garden's variation derives from contrasting combinations of hard landscaping and planting. Birches underplanted with spring bulbs combine with limestone paths to make a sylvan woodland area. A small lawn sets off curved borders of agapanthus, salvias and ornamental grasses augmented with summer annuals.

One intimate courtyard sums up the garden's combination of the traditional and the contemporary. It contains an archway built in traditional wychert (a blend of chalk and clay mixed with straw) with a tile coping. A rough-cast concrete wall forms another side of this courtyard, with a much taller house window just beyond it. A small pool fed by a suggestion of a stream, rocks, a specimen tree with gnarled bark and the textural contrast of herbaceous planting all combine to make this a beautiful stand-alone garden. For the visitor, it is just one of Turn End's many delights.

74

↑　In the walled Mediterranean Garden, an armillary sphere is surrounded by beds of *Papaver orientale* 'Turkish Delight', *Rosa* 'White Pet', foxtail lilies, iris and others.

↓ ↘　Doors fold back to allow an indoor area to spill out on to a terracotta patio beside the pond, which is swathed in lush greenery.

→ [page 76]　A large urn provides a focal point in a border of shade-tolerant planting, including *Hosta* 'Gold Standard' and *Bistorta* spp.

→ [page 77]　The Gravel Garden is full of alpines and dwarf conifers grown in pots.

THE BARN

Tom Stuart-Smith

SERGE HILL,
HERTFORDSHIRE
20th–21st century
2.4 hectares / 6 acres

Tom Stuart-Smith is one of the most intriguing contemporary garden designers, and The Barn is his private house. His hallmark is formal structure softened by exuberant planting, a formula that has characterized British horticulture from the sixteenth to the twenty-first century.

Stuart-Smith brings a touch of the contemporary to this traditional approach. Many of his gardens have an Eastern air, with simple platforms, gravel paths and straight water channels; others follow the recent fashion for grasses and prairie planting. It is in his own personal space that his work is displayed at its quirky best.

In the old farmyard surrounding the converted barn, Stuart-Smith has created a series of dramatic spaces. The cobbled courtyard in front is a combination of lime-green *Euphorbia seguieriana* and purple *Salvia nemorosa*, moderated with a wafty upper layer of yellow *Genista aetnensis*. Threaded through the space are rusted troughs. These water-filled tanks pay homage to the former farmyard and mirror the sky, providing calm in the dense planting.

Behind the barn an old wheat field has been given a framework of yew, beech and hornbeam hedges, creating distinct but interlocking spaces. Some are densely planted; some are left to self-seeders; others are kept as open lawns or grass paths; the rest are flanked by deep flower borders. Over the years Stuart-Smith's plant palette has become increasingly naturalistic, as roses, pinks and peonies have given way to cardoons, thistles and mulleins. Texture and form take precedence over colour, and grasses prevail, with clumps of miscanthus, stipa and calamagrostis providing structure and rhythm while linking the garden to the agricultural landscape. A prairie meadow garden was added in 2011. Stuart-Smith is very tall, and the garden is laid out to his own scale: giant macleaya, hollyhocks, veronicastrum, veronica and fennel create an Alice-in-Wonderland atmosphere, and visitors delight in the anarchy of his idiosyncratic garden.

↓ → *Genista aetnensis* grows in the Courtyard Garden around one of the troughs left from Stuart-Smith's garden for the RHS Chelsea Flower Show in 2006.

↖ Empty green rooms and a long, open lawn provide areas of rest amid the dense planting.

↑ The West Garden was a wheat field twenty years ago. Stuart-Smith has planted hornbeam hedges to create a series of interlinked rooms – some densely planted, others left empty – surrounded by an open meadow of trees and wildflowers.

↓ Developed with advice from James Hitchmough of Sheffield University, the prairie meadow was sown in spring 2011 and began with about forty exotic taxa, which have since been increased.

THE BARN

HATFIELD HOUSE

Salomon de Caus,
6th Marchioness
of Salisbury

HATFIELD, HERTFORDSHIRE
17th, 20th century
17 hectares / 42 acres

↓ The intricate Palace Knot Garden was laid out in the early 1970s with three knots and a maze; the layout and planting were based on Tudor sources.

Hatfield House has a place in English history: an oak tree in the park marks the spot where Elizabeth Tudor learned that she had become queen. The garden preserves not only parts of the Tudor original, but also a highlight of the seventeenth-century English vogue for Mannerist gardens. The greatest champion of the Italian Renaissance style in England was the French engineer Salomon de Caus, who designed gardens filled with complicated hydraulics and magical automata. At Hatfield, de Caus made an elaborate garden for the new house built by Robert Cecil, 1st Earl of Salisbury, in 1607–12.

The formal garden is east of the house, where the land slopes down to the river. The basic layout of 1609 – a terrace leading to an upper garden and thence to a lower one – was actually the work of Cecil's gardener Mountain Jennings. By 1611, however, Jennings had been sacked in favour of the more fashionable de Caus. The current Marchioness has re-created de Caus's design as far as possible.

The Upper Terrace Garden has sixteen formal beds picked out in low box hedges that contain geometric yew topiary and informal plantings of perennials and roses. Lawns set with statuary and topiary lead between the beds, and the garden is flanked by rows of holm oak (*Quercus ilex*) clipped into lollipops. Below, on the second level, is a maze and beyond that an informal pond, both echoes of the original layout. In 1610 Cecil sent his gardener John Tradescant the Elder to Europe to acquire unusual plants for the gardens, including cherries, quince, medlars and Provins roses.

Unusually for the time, Cecil left the old Tudor hall standing. In the 1970s the 6th Marchioness planted a period-correct knot garden in front of it and created a Scented Garden. West of the new house, enclosed by a pleached-lime walk and a yew hedge, is the Privy Garden laid out by Lady Gwendolen, daughter of the 3rd Marquess. Beyond is the Wilderness, a tree collection set in grass full of spring bulbs and wildflowers.

↑ Standard *Lonicera* grows around a sundial, seen here in a heavy hoar frost.

← A large stone bowl acts as a focal point in the Herb Garden west of the house.

↓ Rows of clipped holm oak, *Quercus ilex*, surround the Parterre Garden.

→ [pages 82–83] A dusting of frost lends definition to the Parterre Garden and Hedge Maze in the lower part of the East Garden.

HATFIELD HOUSE

THE BETH CHATTO GARDENS

Beth Chatto

ELMSTEAD MARKET,
ESSEX
20th century
3 hectares / 7 acres

↓ Cool greens from trees and marginal plants set off white arum lilies (*Zantedeschia aethiopica*) and foxgloves.

→ Early-morning sunlight illuminates spring bulbs in the Woodland Garden.

The sheltering conifer hedge at Beth Chatto's garden hides a jewel box of plants in striking and subtle associations. These combinations were informed by Chatto's ecological approach, guided by her husband's research into wild plants. Planting is the focus of the garden, which has little paving or statuary. Here, plants fulfil those roles: a striking white-barked birch (*Betula utilis* var. *jacquemontii*) forms a pivotal focal point, while the tracery of the Mount Etna broom (*Genista aetnensis*) appears lace-like against the sky.

The Gravel Garden is a triumph of sustainable gardening, using plants adapted to the poor soil and dry climate. The paths flow like a dry riverbed, with plants pouring over the sweeping curves. The planting is based on foliage texture and contrast, such as bold bergenia set against fine-leaved *Stipa tenuissima*. Flowers are valued but transient and seed heads, such as those of ornamental onions (*Allium*), used to great effect. Chatto used asymmetrical compositions derived from her study of Japanese flower arranging. Punctuation is provided by vertical stalks of

Verbascum bombyciferum and *Camassia*. From summer onwards, larger mounds are created by the translucent flowers of the giant oat grass (*Stipa gigantea*) and foamy white *Crambe cordifolia*. The plants almost crackle with summer heat, and Mediterranean scents fill the air.

A pollarded English oak (*Quercus robur*) welcomes visitors to the Water Garden, with its stream and cool green lawn. Here the foliage increases dramatically in size. *Gunnera tinctoria* thrives alongside the ponds created by Chatto, and there are dramatic groups of irises and marsh marigolds (*Caltha*).

The Woodland Garden provides a different range of plants. Beneath a canopy of English oaks, the air has an earthy scent and the beds are rich with interest from early spring bulbs, varied hellebores and shade-tolerant shrubs. From there the visitor can see Chatto's nursery, for which the garden is an inspirational 'living catalogue'. Since Chatto's death in 2018, the gardens have remained a family-run business, managed by her granddaughter Julia Boulton.

THE BETH CHATTO GARDENS

← ↓ In the Gravel Garden paths are edged by drought-tolerant plants such as phlomis and *Gladiolus communis* subsp. *byzantinus*.

← Hostas, grasses and ferns spill over a wooden walkway.

→ The focal white-barked birch grows above a lawn bordered by bold-leaved hostas and the finer *Hakonechloa macra* var. *alboaurea*.

THE BETH CHATTO GARDENS

THE GIBBERD GARDEN

Sir Frederick Gibberd

HARLOW, ESSEX
20th century
2.8 hectares / 7 acres

↓   Bright yellow laburnum flowers harmonize with the rich green sward looking towards the Castle, a structure of chopped elm logs Gibberd designed as a plaything for his grandchildren.

The architect, landscape architect and town planner Sir Frederick Gibberd only ever made one garden: that by his house on the outskirts of Harlow New Town (see page 90), for which he became masterplanner in 1946. Gibberd based the town layout on his ability to consult the *genius loci*, and the architect Sylvia Crowe credited him with 'the idea of open space and landscape flowing between compact housing areas'.

The garden, on fields sloping down to a brook, continued to evolve until Gibberd's death in 1984. What he called his 'private pleasure' is highly individual. He wrote: 'The garden became a series of rooms each with its own character, from small intimate spaces to large enclosed prospects.' This was not new, but Gibberd created a garden with a feeling of fluidity. The visitor moves through interlocking spaces – they are too informal to be called 'rooms' – that are both unified and secretive, filled with diversity, contrast, surprise and interesting plants that create drama and excitement. Paths lined with different styles of hedging define the vistas that link the individual experiences.

The compartments themselves are a mix of natural and semi-formal areas, each enlivened with sculptures and *objets trouvés*. Moisture-loving plants, such as *Rheum palmatum*, flank the path of the sylvan walk by the stream. In a grassy glade stands a pair of acanthus-motif Corinthian columns. A sensuous female statue stretches on a cobble-edge stage, backed by an evergreen hedge. The bronze dogs rushing across the lawn look as if they will attack the unwelcome visitor. A twisted cherry tree contrasts with the clean lines of a terracotta pot, but simultaneously the pot's swirling pattern melds with the shadows the branches cast upon it. A Lime Tree Walk leads to a shady concrete gazebo, while the terrace is decorated with pots, sculptures and various Heath Robinson-esque water features. Gibberd's genius is evident throughout in the contrast and diversity that never jar but only build interest.

← ↑ The garden is full of *objets trouvés* and artworks, such as these Corinthian columns and the bronze dogs that lope across the grass.

↓ A statue named Lucinda, carved by the artist Gerda Rubinstein, forms a focal point at the end of a walk of coppiced nut trees.

HARLOW TOWN PARK WATER GARDEN

Dame Sylvia Crowe

HARLOW, ESSEX
20th century
0.4 hectares / 1 acre

The Water Gardens of Harlow were created in 1963–64 by pioneering landscape architect Sylvia Crowe, and in a lasting testament to her ecologically far-sighted approach they are today also home to many native species of flora and fauna. One of the themed areas within the wider 66-hectare (164-acre) informal Harlow Town Park (on which the landscape architect John St Bodfan Gruffydd also worked), the formality of the arrangement of three cobble-banked pools and cascades (restored 2015–17), together with the associated paddling pool and Rhododendron Dell, introduce a delightful and subtle contrast to their naturalistic setting. The elegant white sculpture *Pisces*, reflected so beautifully in the still waters, is one of twelve abstract sculptures by Jesse Watkins based on the signs of the zodiac and was installed in the Water Gardens in 1973. The three pools subsumed existing spring-fed watercress beds, while the park retains the naturally undulating topography and worked-out gravel pits, both demonstrative of Crowe's determination to integrate as many existing landscape features as possible into the substantial 'green wedges' of designed landscape that she ensured flowed between areas of housing on Sir Frederick Gibberd's 1947 masterplan for Harlow New Town (see also page 88).

Crowe was appointed Landscape Consultant to Harlow New Town at its inception, a brief she held for twenty-six years. She described her holistic design approach as 'New Town in the Landscape' rather than 'Landscape in New Towns'. Additionally appointed the Forestry Commission's first landscape consultant in 1964, Crowe is notable for her melding of aesthetic and ecological principles, and her use of the concepts of *genius loci* (the spirit of a place) and borrowed landscapes. She applied these ideas equally effectively to small-scale works, such as the Water Gardens, and to large landscapes for hospitals, power stations, forestry plantations and reservoirs, including Rutland Water, in Leicestershire.

↓ The rectangular pools linked by cascades and edged with cobbles and a gravel path occupy the site of former watercress beds, introducing a contrasting yet harmonious feature within the gently undulating landscape of Harlow Town Park.

↑   From the higher path, the view down over a planted slope draws the eye to the pools and creates a sense of intimacy heightened by the soothing combinations of foliage textures and colours.

→   The planting softens the hard landscaping, producing a harmonious combination within the Water Gardens and creating a visually pleasing transition to the landscape beyond.

↓   Restored between 2015 and 2017, the Water Gardens are a testament to Sylvia Crowe's design skills, which she expressed both on a small garden scale, as here in the elegant planting, and in grand landscapes.

AGA KHAN CENTRE

Madison Cox,
Maki & Associates,
Nelson Byrd Woltz,
Tom Stuart-Smith and Townshend
Landscape Architects, and others

KING'S CROSS, LONDON
21st century
283 sq. metres / 338 sq. yards
(Garden of Life); 98 sq. metres /
117 sq. yards (Garden of Light);
90 sq. metres / 108 sq. yards
(Garden of Tranquillity);
2,200 sq. metres / 2,631 sq. yards:
(Jellicoe Gardens)

↓   Water flows through the *chahar bagh* of the
rooftop Garden of Life by Madison Cox in an
echo of the great gardens of the Mughal Empire
in India, Afghanistan and elsewhere, helping to
create a soothing and stimulating gathering space
for students and staff.

A core component of the Aga Khan Centre (designed by Fumihiko Maki and opened in 2018) and its associated areas is the complex of roof, terrace and courtyard gardens. The gardens vary from small and secluded to larger and exposed, and offer a range of uses from personal contemplation to social interaction. All are contemporary in their design, but all pay homage to the long and diverse heritage of Islamic architecture and garden-making that has been expressed around the world and over the centuries.

Within the Centre itself are six garden spaces; The Garden of Tranquillity, Terrace of Learning, Courtyard of Harmony and Terrace of Discovery are by Maki & Associates. The Garden of Life was designed by Madison Cox, and the Garden of Light by Nelson Byrd Woltz. The key inspirations here are, respectively, the covered loggias found in the Middle East, Persia and Egypt; the courtyards of southern Spain, Morocco and Egypt; the *iwan* – a three-sided outdoor room common in the Middle East and Central Asia; the *talar*, a Persian throne and a place to address a congregation; the great gardens of the Mughal Empire; and the Islamic courtyards of Andalusia. At nearby Victoria Hall (commissioned by His Highness the Aga Khan as student accommodation), the Garden of Reflection and the Terrace of Unity by Vladimir Djurovic Landscape Architecture, respectively draw on the courtyard gardens of Andalusia and Morocco. Completing a 'ribbon' of green spaces are two public areas nearby: the Jellicoe Gardens by Tom Stuart-Smith and Townshend Landscape Architects, which meld Persian and British influences, notably the Bagh-e Fin garden in Kashan, Iran, and Persian orchards; and the Lewis Cubitt Square by OLIN and Townshend Landscape Architects, which features elements shared by many global garden styles, although the fifty-five water sprays are of Islamic inspiration. Key unifiers of all these gardens are architectural elements, geometric patterns, hard surfaces and water, all arranged symmetrically.

→ The pale limestone floor reflects light and draws the eye to the central fountain in the Garden of Tranquillity by Maki & Associates. Enclosed on three sides, it offers a vista over the Jellicoe Gardens in a way similar to covered loggias of the Middle East, Persia and Egypt.

↓ Inspired by the Islamic courtyards of Andalusia in Spain, the Garden of Light by Nelson Byrd Woltz is bordered by patterned screens featuring a ribbon of marble inscribed with poetry by celebrated Persian poets, and extracts from the Qur'an. The octagonal pool and trees evoke Seville's Patio de los Naranjos (orange grove).

→ [pages 94–95] Named after Sir Geoffrey Jellicoe, a leading twentieth-century British landscape architect, and designed by Tom Stuart-Smith, the Jellicoe Gardens are an English take on a Persian *bustan* or orchard. The rill in the middle of the path flows from a pool set within the airy pavilion, and the beds either side are planted for year-round interest.

BARBICAN
CONSERVATORY
& GARDENS

Chamberlin, Powell
and Bon, Nigel Dunnett

LONDON
20th–21st century
1.5 hectares / 3.7 acres

↓   Grasses of different heights and forms, including blue oat grass (*Helictotrichon sempervirens*) and *Sesleria nitida*, dominate the steppe environments.

→   As well as softening the Brutalist architecture, carefully choreographed plantings add splashes of controlled colour 'eruptions' throughout the year. Here, the early-summer purple is *Allium* 'Globemaster' and *A.* 'Purple Sensation'.

Begun in the 1950s, the Barbican Centre is the largest performing arts complex in Europe. Designed by Chamberlin, Powell and Bon, its Brutalist design incorporates three ornamental gardens: the Lake Terrace, the Conservatory and the Beech Gardens.

The enclosed lake is enlivened with cascades and fountains. Perched in the sky atop the theatre's fly tower, the Conservatory's concrete infrastructure is softened by the varied greens of foliage and the sculptural forms of tropical plants. Complementing the lush plantings are pools filled with exotic fish.

Designed primarily for residents, the Beech Gardens (a roof garden) are nonetheless publicly accessible. In 2013 the high maintenance, water-demanding flower beds, shrubs, trees and lawn were replaced by

Nigel Dunnett with three 'Designed Plant Communities': combinations of plants that are ecologically compatible and imitate natural plant ecosystems, designed to suit the site's different microclimates. Covering the largest area is Steppe Planting, using plants adapted to dry, exposed conditions. The mixture of grasses and perennials was selected for diverse foliage, forms and textures, and to present a show of jewel-like colours. Shrub Steppe Planting contains low-density shrubs and multi-stemmed trees as well to introduce height and create year-round structure and interest. Light Woodland Planting experiences partial shade. Multi-stemmed trees form a light, open canopy, beneath which is an understorey of shrubs; at the lowest level is a rich mix of perennials.

BARBICAN CONSERVATORY & GARDENS

↑ The Shrub Steppe Planting extends the dry-adapted grasslands or meadow to include a scattering of shrubs and small trees.

↗ In early and midsummer, the steppe plantings transform, as spring bulbs give way to summer flowers. Here, purple alliums, silvery grasses and yellow-green *Euphorbia characias* subsp. *wulfenii* bring an architectural element to the planting.

→ Opened in 1984, the Conservatory houses a mix of plants from various habitats, with tree ferns, date palms, Swiss cheese plant, coffee and ginger under one roof. The Arid House, attached to the Conservatory, hosts a collection of cacti and succulents and an overwintering collection of *Cymbidium* orchids.

↓ The autumn show is dominated by foliage in various hues, combined with interesting and contrasting forms and textures.

BARBICAN CONSERVATORY & GARDENS

HANDS OFF MANGROVE GARDEN

Grow2Know,
Tayshan Hayden-Smith,
Danny Clarke

LONDON
21st century
70 sq. metres / 84 sq. yards

↓ Originally designed for the RHS Chelsea Flower Show before its relocation to North Kensington, the 'Hands Off Mangrove' garden was sponsored by the charity Project Giving Back.

↘ A medley of *Astrantia major* 'Pink Pride', *Agapanthus* 'White Pixie' and *Salvia nemerosa* 'Crystal Blue' abut a pool near the entrance of the garden.

Hands Off Mangrove is a community garden with pedigree. Originally commissioned in 2022 from the not-for-profit organization Grow2Know for the RHS Chelsea Flower Show, the internationally recognized showcase for cutting-edge planting and design, it is currently undergoing relocation to a permanent home in west London. The garden is designed to highlight the plight of ecologically important mangrove forests as well as the story of the Mangrove Nine, a group of activists who were tried for and acquitted of inciting a riot at a 1970 protest, taking on the might of the British state.

A 4-metre (13-foot) tall corten steel sculpture by the artist Rob Olins straddles the garden matched with tall, pollarded willows and nestled in colourful textural planting. Paths made from recycled concrete lead to a central space that offers a sanctuary in the heart of the city. London is an urban heat island, and the plant palette takes advantage of this microclimate, incorporating a medley of vibrant and pollinator-friendly plants. Alliums, lupins, plume thistles and the dark foliage of *Verbena macdougalii* 'Lavender Spires' are woven with diaphanous flowers such as *Orlaya grandiflora* and bright aquilegias in boisterous, pick-and-mix combinations. In the tradition of community gardening, edibles – including beetroot, peppers, rocket and tomatoes – are planted in tubs to encourage picking and eating.

The ethos of the garden is one of resilience, with accessibility at its core. Designers Tayshan Hayden-Smith and Danny Clarke deliberately used only those plants available from nurseries at the point of planting. (Typically, plants for an RHS Chelsea garden are grown to order, starting more than a year beforehand.) The result is an immersive garden packed full of lively planting, welcoming to all and pleasingly biodiverse. The garden was awarded an RHS Silver-gilt Medal.

↑   A central steel structure has nine 'roots' representing the Mangrove Nine, a group of black activists who confronted discrimination and racism by protesting against police brutality at the Mangrove Restaurant in North Kensington in 1970.

↓   A sheltered seating spot is surrounded by plants that nod towards a mangrovian theme but will thrive in their west London location.

→   *Lupinus* 'Masterpiece', *Eschscholzia californica* 'Orange King', *Geranium psilostemon* and *Cirsium rivulare* 'Atropurpureum' create layers of texture and colour.

ROYAL BOTANIC GARDENS, KEW

William Kent,
Lancelot 'Capability' Brown
and others

RICHMOND, LONDON
18th–21st century
121.5 hectares / 300 acres

↓ The famed Palm House was built in the mid-nineteenth century to house the many different types of palm being brought back from all parts of the British Empire.

Kew is not the world's first botanic garden: that is in Pisa. Nor is it England's oldest: that title belongs to the one at Oxford University (1621). It is, however, the world's premier botanic garden, a status it has held since its foundation as such in the last quarter of the eighteenth century. But the history of Kew as a plant collection began in the 1660s, when Sir Henry Capel established his botanical rarities and exotics around Kew House. In 1730 Frederick, Prince of Wales, leased the house and had William Kent lay out the grounds. Upon Frederick's death in 1751, his widow, Augusta, teamed up with the Earl of Bute to create a large Physic Garden.

In 1760 King George III acquired Kew House, and it became a refuge during his bouts of 'insanity' (he suffered from porphyria). He united the grounds with those of another royal residence, Richmond Lodge, and asked 'Capability' Brown to design the enlarged landscape. However, it was Joseph Banks in the 1770s – lately returned from circumnavigating the world with Captain (then Lieutenant) James Cook – who established Kew as a world centre for the study of botany. He sent plant-hunters around the world to develop the collections, organized the study of their discoveries and arranged to transport economically important plants between British colonies.

Kew's elegant grounds and plant collections are beautiful all year round. Highlights include William Chambers' Chinese-inspired Pagoda; the renowned glasshouse; the Rhododendron Dell (part of Brown's landscape); the Rock Garden; and the arboretum. Particular features are the Palm House (1848) and the Temperate House (1863), designed by Decimus Burton, and the Princess of Wales Conservatory (1987).

It is possible to spend days at Kew soaking up the history and beauty. Yet Kew is still a scientific institution at the very cutting edge of botany, helping in the fight against the global loss of biodiversity.

↖ At the end of vista is the ten-storey octagonal Pagoda built by William Chambers in 1762. A single cedar of Lebanon (*Cedrus liban*) blocks the view – but it is such a fine specimen that it has been left in place.

↑ The focus of the Woodland Garden, the Temple of Aeolus is framed in spring by the flowers of magnolias and camellias.

↓ *Dicksonia antarctica*, native to Australia, thrives in the Temperate House, the largest Victorian glass structure in the world.

HAMPTON COURT PALACE

Henry VIII,
André Mollet,
George London,
Daniel Marot

EAST MOLESEY, SURREY
16th–20th century
24.3 hectares / 60 acres

↓ The Privy Garden has been restored to its appearance of 1702. The elaborate *parterres à l'anglais,* contain 33,000 box plants.

Hampton Court Palace was gifted to Henry VIII by Cardinal Wolsey in 1529 and the king turned it into the last word in power gardening that included a Privy Garden full of heraldic devices. Today the sunken Pond Gardens, filled in spring with tulips and in summer with bedding plants, are the sole survivor but part of Henry's Privy Garden has been re-created on the former Chapel Court Garden. In the seventeenth century, the Privy Garden was successively modified by Charles I, Oliver Cromwell and Charles II, who also had André Mollet lay out a new garden in the latest French fashion (the Long Water is a surviving feature).

For William III and Mary II, George London and Daniel Marot reworked the gardens into an ornate Dutch-inspired Baroque style, between 1690 and 1702, and the Privy Garden acquired the layout to which it has now been restored. The scrollwork lawns set within gravel paths are known as *parterre à l'anglaise.* The Privy Garden is the perfect foil to the south front of the palace

extension designed by Sir Christopher Wren from 1689. Against the east facade the layout of William and Mary's garden remains, with clipped yew trees lining the three avenues of the *patte d'oie* (goose's foot) that pierce a semicircular area at the building's centre. This semicircle would have featured ornate, Dutch-inspired *parterres de broderie,* but today it consists of lawn studded with Victorian-inspired bedding displays. The main axis leads to the Long Water. A third feature from the William and Mary era is the last vestige of the Wilderness Garden created in the Dutch style to the north of the palace.

The famous maze was planted in 1690 as a form of courtly entertainment. Meanwhile, near the Pond Gardens, a modern glasshouse has been erected over the Great Vine – *Vitis vinifera* 'Schiava Grossa' (also known as 'Black Hamburgh') – which was planted in 1768 by 'Capability' Brown when he was royal gardener to George III. The vine still bears fruit in early autumn.

→ In spring the Pond Garden brims with tulips. The garden once had citrus trees grown in tubs, but was filled with bedding plants in Victorian times.

↓ Clipped yew (*Taxus baccata*) makes a strong geometric arrangement at the apex of a *patte d'oie* of avenues looking towards the Long Water and Home Park.

HAMPTON COURT PALACE

MUNSTEAD WOOD

Gertrude Jekyll

BUSBRIDGE, GODALMING,
SURREY
19th–20th century
4 hectares / 10 acres

Gertrude Jekyll was arguably the most influential British garden designer of the twentieth century, and she used her own garden at Munstead Wood to develop her ideas. Her partnership with the architect Edwin Lutyens, who designed the house, created a new British garden style. This Arts and Crafts style was characterized by using local materials in local ways and by employing inventive geometry to define and link areas filled with profuse yet carefully ordered planting. Jekyll was a plantswoman par excellence and the first to apply painterly colour theory to flower-bed design.

Jekyll bought the triangular plot in 1882 and began work on the garden while living across the road with her mother. Lutyens slotted the house into the space that was left; it was finished in 1897.

The outlying area is an ornamental woodland. Jekyll allowed five local heath species to regenerate: silver birch, holly, beech, Scots pine and Spanish chestnut. Each was underplanted with different shrubs and colourful flowers, of which perhaps the most spectacular are the springtime displays of rhododendrons and azaleas.

North of the house, linking it to the garden, is the shady North Court, with steps leading past a water tank. From the court, the Nut Walk, flanked by shrubs and the Aster Garden, leads to a rose-covered pergola. At the west end of the Nut Walk is the garden's most famous feature. Backed by a wall covered with climbers and wall-trained shrubs is the long Main Border. Jekyll colour-choreographed this iconic border, with pale, cool-coloured flowers at each end building to hot reds and yellows at the centre. Through the arch in the wall are the Spring and Summer gardens, with displays including tulips, irises and peonies, and to the west of the house lies the sunken Rock Garden.

Munstead Wood was sold in 1948 and the plot divided, but it remains one of the most important twentieth-century British gardens. The house and garden are now privately owned, and the current owners have done much to restore the garden to its original form and planting.

↓ A paved area near the house features a water tank/pond and is planted with spheres of box (*Buxus*) and red pelargoniums.

← An arched gate leads through the Main Border into the Spring Garden with a wall swathed in climbing roses.

↓ The Aster Garden is a mass of purples and pinks in front of the characteristic Lutyens house.

→ [pages 108–109] The hot-colour border features red-hot poker (*Kniphofia uvaria*) with cannas, dahlias and gladioli.

BALMORAL COTTAGE

Charlotte Molesworth

BENENDEN,
NEAR CRANBROOK, KENT
20th–21st century
0.4 hectares/1 acre (garden);
2 hectares / 5 acres (wider landscape)

↓ The garden at Balmoral Cottage is an enclosed world of magical, topiarized delights created mainly from yew (*Taxus baccata*), box (*Buxus sempervirens*), holly (*Ilex* sp.) and hornbeam (*Carpinus betulus*).

The eclectic, eccentric garden of artist and designer Charlotte Molesworth is best known for its topiary. In the Weald of Kent, Molesworth has clipped and shaped a fantastical world of peacocks, dogs, chickens, cones and helical swirls, mostly in box and yew. Each piece of topiary in the garden is clipped in response to the natural growth of its host. Molesworth encourages natural shapes in the branches of a shrub with judicious pruning, canes and string. After 40 years, the result is a magical, quirky garden that is intimate and atmospheric.

The garden is located in the village of Benenden in Kent, on the site of a former kitchen garden owned by the Victorian plant hunter Collingwood 'Cherry' Ingram. Ingram earned his nickname from his passion for flowering cherries. Almost every plant has been nurtured from seed, seedling or cutting. Charlotte requested yew seedlings from friends as wedding presents and took box cuttings from her mother's garden, buying only a handful of young box plants at the start.

Three quarters of the garden has been cultivated, the rest is wild with plum trees, blackthorn and brambles to benefit wildlife. There is also a generous vegetable patch, a glasshouse and a nuttery, as well as space for a donkey, sheep, chickens and bees, yet the garden was created without a masterplan. Bold hedges do the practical job of reducing the wind across the site and dividing the garden as well as highlighting its central vista, but overall, its design is a result of incremental decisions. Thrift is a central theme; bricks reclaimed from the original 1980s edging around Cherry's kitchen garden have been used to make the floors in the house. Paths are made with factory seconds or are laid to grass with stable blocks as stepping stones. A collection of vintage watering cans nestles by the door, and plastic citrus barrels are reused as water butts. This is a garden that was ahead of its time in its reduce, reuse recycle approach.

↑   The topiary is softened by old-fashioned, cottage garden favourites. The skyline is as much a part of the garden as the planting.

↙↓   Everything in the garden has been grown from scratch or creatively rescued and repurposed. Buying is the not first thing that comes to mind.

PROSPECT COTTAGE

Derek Jarman

DUNGENESS, KENT
20th century
Approximately 0.4 hectares / 1 acre

Filmmaker Derek Jarman's garden is one of the smallest yet most magical in this book. Decades after his death, it is still a cult destination on the bleak shingle headland at Dungeness. Created over eight years, it combines colourful planting with rusted metal 'sculptures' and arrangements of weathered driftwood and flint. Many of the plants are native to the landscape, so can tolerate the salt-laden winds, strong sun and low rainfall. There are stands of green broom, with purple sea kale, sea pea, cotton lavender and elder (traditionally planted as protection from witches). Jarman also introduced some species. Summer colours come from white pinks, red poppies, marigolds, irises and blue cornflower; in autumn the palette is brown and skeletal grey from wood, lichens and mosses.

The front garden has a formal element, with two 1.2-metre (4-foot) circles of concentric flints and bricks, plus a similar oblong, all inspired by Jarman's interest in leylines.

The planting at the back is more random, with scattered opium poppy, valerian, foxglove and viper's bugloss. There are no fences, so it is difficult to say where the garden ends. Pillars of driftwood rise above the vegetation like sentinels, some staking dog rose or gorse, the honeyed scent of which surrounds the visitor.

On the south wall of the cottage are lines from John Donne's poem 'The Sunne Rising', lending the garden a poignancy linked with Jarman's early death in 1994. Jarman created the garden in the shadow of the Dungeness nuclear reactor as therapy after being diagnosed with HIV. He took as inspiration Gertrude Jekyll (see page 106) and his friends Beth Chatto and Christopher Lloyd (see pages 84 and 120). In this, he succeeded so fully that, even now, the garden remains true to its maker's magical and profoundly humane vision. In 2020 the cottage and garden were acquired by the Art Fund for the nation; Creative Folkestone is now the custodian.

↓   In front of the cottage, clumps of poppies, marigolds and other summer flowers obscure Jarman's formal circles of flints and shingle.

↑ *Crambe maritima* (sea kale) grows next to a sculptural arrangement made from driftwood with flints and found pieces of iron.

↗ Among the columns of driftwood in the less formal back garden, the wind has fashioned tight clumps of artemisia, cotton lavender, cistus, roses, sage and sea kale.

↓ A circle of viper's bugloss surrounds a clump of lavender in one of the stone circles in the front garden.

→ California poppies (*Eschscholzia californica*) bloom beside a circle of flints carefully sorted by colour.

SISSINGHURST CASTLE GARDEN

Harold Nicolson,
Vita Sackville-West,
Dan Pearson

SISSINGHURST, NEAR
CRANBROOK, KENT
20th, 21st century
4 hectares / 10 acres

↓   Views from the tower of the South
Cottage and the Rondel Rose Garden reveal
how Nicolson's structural framework melds
with Sackville-West's exuberant plantings.

→   The tower rises behind daffodils in the
orchard in early spring; the orchard also
features a classical altar and a dovecot.

Sissinghurst Castle has one of the most quintessentially English and influential gardens of the twentieth century. The configuration of 'rooms', each with its own character, reflects the personalities of its creators, Vita Sackville-West and Harold Nicolson. As individuals they led fascinating lives; together they created a garden that is greater than the sum of their two characters.

Sackville-West made the garden famous through her writings, and often (unfairly) receives all the credit. Certainly each of the nine rooms is a masterpiece demonstrating her skills as a plantswoman and designer. But the garden as a whole is a fusion of her romantic heart and Nicolson's classical mind. For it was Nicolson who gave the garden structure and form, carving out from the asymmetric plot a series of compartments divided by red-brick walls and tall hedges of clipped yew. They are linked visually by vistas and physically by stone- or red-brick-flagged paths and many are subdivided into

beds by low, neat hedges of box. The Delos garden, a failed attempt to design a sun-drenched Greek garden, was finally created by Dan Pearson (see page 166) in 2021.

Made in the decade before World War II, the garden nods respectfully to the work of another partnership – that of Gertrude Jekyll and Edwin Lutyens (see page 160) – in particular in the use of rooms and colour-themed planting. Yet it is more personal and more romantic than a typical Jekyll and Lutyens garden. It is clothed with abundance and abandon, with choreographed colours that harmonize, contrast and blend, and it demonstrates a passion for roses. As Sackville-West noted, the garden has a 'profusion, even extravagance and exuberance, within confines of the utmost linear severity'. While it is a big garden by most standards, Sissinghurst has enduring appeal because each room is (relatively) small and intimate and there is always some small vignette or idea the visitor can try at home.

→ The Cottage Garden is filled with red, orange and yellow flowers: tulips and wallflowers in spring (seen here); goldenrod and helenium in summer.

↓ In the Herb Garden, sedum and houseleeks grow in a marble bowl in front of cannas, roses and low-growing herbs. At the back is yellow *Rudbeckia laciniata* 'Herbstsonne'.

↑ ↓ →   The White Garden is at its best in late June and July, when the *Rosa mulliganii* flowers on the central iron trellis. Masses of white or grey plants, such as *Crambe cordifolia*, variegated phlox and artemesia, are framed by dark box, while a willow-leaved pear (*Pyrus salicifolia* 'Pendula') shades a statue by the sculptor Toma Rosandić.

→ [pages 118–119]   With its drystone raised beds, rocky ornaments, gnarled olive trees and predominantly Greek flora, the Delos garden by Dan Pearson (with advice from Olivier Filippi) opened in 2020 and reinterprets Sackville-West and Nicholson's vision of the garden that was inspired by a visit to that island in 1935.

SISSINGHURST CASTLE GARDEN

GREAT DIXTER

Sir Edwin Lutyens, Nathaniel Lloyd,
Christopher Lloyd, Fergus Garrett

NORTHIAM, RYE,
EAST SUSSEX
20th–21st century
2 hectares / 5 acres

Although Great Dixter is associated with the *enfant terrible* of twentieth-century horticulture, Christopher Lloyd, the bones of the garden were created a century ago by his parents and Sir Edwin Lutyens, who devised the overall layout and incorporated a barn and oast house into the design as boundaries, using cattle drinking troughs as decorative pools and the cowshed as a loggia. Over fifty years the younger Lloyd (known as Christo) transformed the Arts and Crafts garden into a palette for contemporary ideas, having inherited his love of gardening from his mother, Daisy, who had an informal style.

Lloyd's father, Nathaniel, created a series of hedged enclosures around the old farmyard. He also created several topiary birds – which all came to resemble abstract peacocks – and the Sunk Garden with its octagonal pool, created from the flat lawn in Lutyen's Barn garden.

Aged thirty-three, having studied for a horticultural degree, Christo returned to live with his widowed mother. Over the years he softened his father's design with luxuriant planting. Extending the 40-metre (130-foot) Long Border by a third, he replaced the tasteful Jekyll-esque colours with striking combinations such as red tulips and lime-green euphorbia. Fascinated by form and texture, he incorporated unusual plants, among them cannas, yuccas and miscanthus. One of the first gardeners in England to adopt the loose 'perennial' style, he promoted meadow gardens and pioneered succession planting to ensure interest all year round. Late in life, he outraged the horticultural community by replacing the Rose Garden with an exotic garden of dramatic plants: Japanese banana (*Musa basjoo*), Polynesian elephant ear (*Colocasia*) and the tall grass *Arundo donax*.

A true plantsman, Lloyd shared his prodigious knowledge through lectures, books and newspaper columns, helping to make Great Dixter one of the most loved of England's modern gardens. Today, the house and garden are owned by a charitable trust, and head gardener Fergus Garrett continues Lloyd's legacy.

↓   The artfully planted Long Border, the most famous part of the garden, is a striking contrast to the meadow beside it.

↑ Formerly a rose garden, today the Exotic garden is filled with exuberant planting, using plants like ferns, bamboos, yucca, and the hardy Japanese banana plant, *Musa basjoo*, to name a few.

↙ In spring the Orchard Garden is bright with *Tulipa* 'West Point' and forget-me-nots (*Myosotis* 'Blue Ball').

↓ The garden retains its sculptural form even in winter. Seen here is the octagonal pool of the Sunk Garden.

→ [pages 122–123] An elevated view shows how yew hedges give structure to the High Garden; in the foreground are the topiary peacocks created by Christopher Lloyd's father, Nathaniel.

GREAT DIXTER

DENMANS

Joyce Robinson,
John Brookes

FONTWELL, ARUNDEL,
WEST SUSSEX
20th century
1.6 hectares / 4 acres

↓   Expanses of lawn are balanced by large
areas of mixed planting that are anchored
by trees and larger shrubs.

→   The gravel 'river' of the Dry Stream
Garden flows beneath a stone 'bridge',
past graceful silver birches and *Euphorbia*.

Denmans is an outstanding example of modern garden design. The large space feels domestic in scale, and there are plenty of design principles and planting ideas to absorb. Joyce Robinson, who started gardening there in 1946, was a keen plantswoman and an innovative gardener. A visit to Greece in 1969 inspired her to use gravel as a ground surface and as a mulch around plants.

In 1980 John Brookes brought his School of Garden Design to Denmans, and the garden evolved as a workshop for his design philosophy. Through his books and teaching, Brookes became one of Britain's most influential landscape designers. There are no straight lines, no formal axes leading to focal points, and few traditional paths. Curving lawns appear to blend into large areas of planting and gravel paths. Spatial layout is achieved through the placement of plant masses – of trees and larger shrubs – balanced with void areas of lawn, gravel and low planting. Shape and leaf form, texture

and colour make as big an impact as more transient flower colour. Brookes acknowledged the influence of Thomas Church, the Modernist Californian landscape architect. Seeing the garden as an outdoor room is another concept Brookes originally championed in his extremely influential book *Room Outside* (1969).

Denmans is a garden to be enjoyed. Seats are placed in sunny positions, and areas of grass are left longer, with low-maintenance paths mown through. Expanses of lawn encourage visitors to explore; a gravel 'stream' flows under a large stone bridge into a real pond. Large empty pots act as focal points or as accents on the edge of plant groups.

The garden can be enjoyed via a variety of routes, each revealing different discoveries. For plant-lovers, the taller plant groups and lower-growing plant associations are noteworthy. Brookes' use of materials offers an invaluable lesson for designers and gardeners alike.

← In the Walled Garden, *Rheum palmatum* grows in a mixed border with tulips and euphorbia.

↑ *Astelia chathamica* and *Eryngium* grow beside a large urn in a circle of gravel.

↓ Wide gravel and railway-sleeper steps allow space for people and plants, including *Verbascum olympicum*, *Sisyrinchium striatum* and foxgloves.

GRAVETYE MANOR

William Robinson,
Tom Coward

EAST GRINSTEAD,
WEST SUSSEX
19th–20th, 21st century
12.1 hectares / 30 acres

↓   Naturalistic planting softens the straight lines of the paths and the house's walls.

→   The Flower Garden, a series of stone terraces, was home to the first modern mixed border, planted by Robinson in 1884.

Gravetye Manor belonged to William Robinson, a leading late nineteenth-century garden writer and protagonist of what became known as the 'Battle of Styles', an acrimonious debate about the future of British gardening. Robinson, who acquired the sixteenth century manor in 1884, wanted to move Victorian fashions away from the formal Italianate garden towards a more naturalistic style filled with hardy plants. He used Gravetye to put his ideas into practice. Following two decades of neglect after his death in 1935, the house became a hotel and the gardens were restored.

Robinson's dogmatic approach upset many, notably the architect Reginald Blomfield. Blomfield also wanted to see a new form of garden, but he preferred a return to Renaissance formality. Their broadsides led to the evolution of a new style created by Gertrude Jekyll and Edwin Lutyens (see page 160).

Gravetye's Wild Garden provides a good display of the Robinsonian method. Grass paths wind through meadows where bulbs, annuals and perennials have naturalized. There are ornamental shrubs and trees, including Corsican pines and a handkerchief tree (*Davidia involucrata*), which appear natural rather than deliberately planted.

Robinson was not shy of hypocrisy: he laid out the existing terrace garden as a formal flower garden. Today it is a lawn flanked by mixed borders with views over the Wildflower Meadow. There the seasonal show begins with snowdrops and crocuses, which give way to *Scilla siberica* and wild daffodils. Bluebells and *Anemone nemorosa* 'Robinsoniana' flower next, and in early summer come native wildflowers, including thousands of common spotted orchids. After mowing, the meadow's last flourish is of autumn crocuses. In contrast, the Flower Garden's rustic terraces are informally planted with deciduous azaleas that provide glorious flowers in late spring and striking foliage in autumn. Today the head gardener, Tom Coward, works his magic in the garden.

↓   The straight lines of the flagged path are softened by cheerful planting, and steps lead the visitor to an ebullient floral show beyond.

→   The tutti-frutti mix of tulips bring a splash of warm colours to a spring border, while the blue of forget-me-nots introduces a cool contrast.

→ [pages 130–131]   The mix of formal and informal components in the garden, so typical of Robinson, is clear when viewed from above. The unusually shaped oval kitchen garden provides produce for the hotel restaurant. The walls, of local Sussex sandstone, were built from 1898 to 1901, and the current owners take great pride in preserving this heritage garden.

←   The pergola at the garden's terminus frames views out over the borrowed landscape, while an underplanting of lavender adds its distinctive perfume.

↑   A new, seasonally planted boundary border by Tom Coward, here with alliums, links the formality of the pergola with the informality of the meadow beyond.

→   Native wild daffodils (*Narcissus pseudonarcissus*) flourish in the meadow.

BURY COURT

John Coke, Piet Oudolf,
Christopher Bradley-Hole

BENTLEY, FARNHAM,
SURREY
20th–21st century
2,600 sq. metres / 3,110 sq. yards

↓   An abstract landscape of formal simplicity,
designed by Christopher Bradley-Hole, is one
half of the garden at Bury Court.

It is unusual to find a garden of two halves that has been designed by two different garden designers. The Courtyard behind Bury Court was designed by Piet Oudolf in 1997, in collaboration with the garden's former owner, the nurseryman John Coke, in what was Oudolf's first British garden commission. In 2002 the front garden was designed by Christopher Bradley-Hole. The house, barn and a trio of oast houses sit in the middle of the two.

Oudolf's planting in the Courtyard typifies his early work, with bold, oversized, geometric domes and swirls of topiary in box and yew and sweeps of perennials and grasses. Notable is his use of the same supersized drifts of planting that he uses in his large-scale works in this, a relatively small, domestic garden. In the front garden, Christopher Bradley-Hole's pared-back, abstract design similarly uses herbaceous perennials and grasses. In a dreamlike space, predominantly tall grasses, such as *Calamagrostis* ×

acutiflora 'Karl Foerster' and *Miscanthus sinensis* are arranged in a grid of twenty rusted steel-edged beds. The garden is crisscrossed by straight paths of bound gravel and granite setts that echo the materials of the house, mainly brick and clunch (a chalky limestone), to create a minimalist, harmonious design. As the seasons change the grasses grow and billow, subverting the strict formality of the garden's layout. The result is an acutely immersive, enveloping space. Later in the year, the greens turn golden and are dotted with red sanguisorba flowers.

At the centre of the garden is a weathered-oak pavilion, also designed by Bradley Hole, abutted by a rectangular, reflective pool. The square structure of the pavilion reflects the grid-like pattern of the garden, and viewed from within, the spaces between its posts frame views of the Hampshire countryside. The pool is blackened to increase its reflectivity and draw the sky down into the garden.

↑ Inspired by Bradley-Hole's design in the front garden, this area of the garden was designed by John Coke and features geometric blocks of *Calamagrostis × acutiflora* 'Karl Foerster' (reed grass), seen here glowing golden in early autumn.

↓ Carefully rationed flowers and seed heads are matched with geometric topiary in the Courtyard, designed by Piet Oudolf.

EXBURY GARDENS

Lionel de Rothschild,
Edmund de Rothschild

EXBURY, SOUTHAMPTON,
HAMPSHIRE
20th century
101 hectares / 250 acres

Exbury, one of England's finest woodland gardens, is best known for its important collections of rhododendrons and azaleas. The woodland was planted largely to provide these collections with protection from salty winds blowing up the river from the Solent. The garden was created by Lionel Nathan de Rothschild between 1919 and his death in 1942. A member of the famous banking family, he was once described as 'a banker by hobby and a gardener by profession'.

Rothschild's abiding passion was for rhododendrons (the genus now includes azaleas), and he went to considerable lengths to populate his garden. As well as buying new cultivars and breeding his own, including the Exbury hybrids, Rothschild was a major sponsor of plant-hunters who scoured Burma and the Himalayas for new species. He also had a strong influence on Ambrose Congreve and his garden at Mount Congreve in Ireland.

After Rothschild's death, his son Edmund expanded and developed Exbury. He repaired the damage suffered in World War II bombing raids – the garden is close to the port city of Southampton – and opened the gardens to the public in 1955. His brother, Leopold, also added a narrow-gauge railway, which transports visitors to the northeastern corner of the garden.

Today there is more to Exbury than rhododendrons. The season begins in the early spring, when the Daffodil Meadow is a field of gold and the woodland is abloom with magnolias and camellias (there are more than 250 different types of the latter, including Lionel's hybrids). In mid-spring, when the wood is carpeted with bluebells and primroses, the show of 10,000 flowering rhododendrons and azaleas reaches its peak, most dramatically in the stunning Azalea Bowl. Summer is the season to enjoy both the Herbaceous and Grasses Garden and the Exotic Garden, while autumn brings fiery foliage from maple, deciduous azalea and dogwood. This time of year is also the chance to enjoy Exbury's collection of nerine and the National Collections of tupelo (*Nyssa*) and sourwood (*Oxydendrum*) trees.

↓ → Exbury is home to many remarkable specimens. In May the Spring Garden offers a spectacular display of colourful maples (*Acer*) and azaleas.

↙ ↓ Water is an integral part of the garden, with streams threading their way through the woodland past azaleas, maples, *Gunnera*, umbrella plants (*Darmera peltata*) and wild garlic.

FRANKLIN FARM

Kim Wilkie,
Pip Morrison

**BISHOP'S WALTHAM,
HAMPSHIRE**
16th, 21st century
14.2 hectares / 35 acres

↓ At Franklin Farm a serpentine ha-ha links
the meadow and the house with the pasture.

Franklin Farm is a 35-acre smallholding in the Hampshire Downs worked by landscape architects Kim Wilkie and Pip Morrison. The farm follows ancient traditions of growing food and fuel in collaboration with nature, and every element of the garden has quiet purpose and is carefully considered.

The smallholding sits in a wider chalk landscape. It is edged with 4 hectares (10 acres) of woodland, including oak, beech and field maple trees that were planted in the 1990s, following the contours of the land. A half-mile bumpy track leads to the farm. At the back of a fifteenth-century farmhouse and outbuildings in wood and flint, they have created a sunken, spiral grass landform designed to display a sculpture by the Bristol artist Simon Thomas. The spoils from its excavation have been used to create a spiral grass mound in the field behind, from the top of which, on a clear day, it is possible to see Tennyson Down on the Isle of Wight.

In front of the property, Morrison's double herbaceous borders burst with colour and life. Vibrant cottage-garden favourites, such as phlox, penstemon, hollyhock, roses and lurching delphiniums abound, woven with well chosen self-seeders such as ammi and poppies in huge swathes of mesmerizing planting.

Next to the threshing barn is a walled garden with nine geometric beds and a terrace of flint and brick, planted in the cool greens and pale yellow of hostas, eryngium, white valerian and soft yellow daylilies among others. A number of the plants have been allowed to self-seed gently, filling the cracks in the walls and paths. There is a circular dew pond close to the house and a vibrant vegetable garden. A curving ha-ha hidden in long grass connects the grazing land with the garden.

Franklin Farm has been in Wilkie's family since 1961, when his parents bought it as an abandoned property while living overseas. Today it is an idyllic garden in perfect isolation, deftly designed by a pair of modern creatives.

↖ Everything is productive, from the orchard and vegetable plot to the wider smallholding. Growing food, poultry, livestock and wildlife are all integrated.

↑ The circular dew pond, with marginal planting to benefit wildlife, was restored in the 1990s and connects to the grazed landscape beyond.

↓ Earthworks echo Bronze Age history. The sculpture is by Bristol artist Simon Thomas.

MAGGIE'S CENTRE GARDEN

Sarah Price

SOUTHAMPTON, HAMPSHIRE
21st century
0.2 hectares / 0.5 acres

The garden designed by Sarah Price at Maggie's Centre, Southampton, is based on a woodland glade, inspired by the ecology of the nearby New Forest. Being in nature has a positive impact on how we feel, and Maggie's Southampton is one of a number of cancer support centres in the UK that feature a design-led garden.

Located on the former car park at Southampton NHS Foundation Trust hospital, the garden wraps around an earth-toned ceramic and mottled stainless steel-clad building designed by the architects AL_A. The dappled, mirrored surfaces reflect the greens of the garden. Visitors approach through a birch woodland underplanted with mosses, ferns and other woodland flora. Wood anemones, orchids, wild garlic, bluebells and primroses all inch across the woodland paths, creating a pocket forest. Trees, rather than sculpture, are the focal points. Multi-stemmed birch

(*Betula pendula*) and expressively shaped *Amelanchier × lamarckii* are arranged in borders no more than 3 metres (10 feet) wide. A ruddy-barked Tibetan cherry (*Prunus serrula*) provides colour, and Scots pine trees, the traditional wayfaring trees that are used to mark safe ground in the landscape, will eventually grow taller than the building, marking its location.

At the perimeter of the garden the land rises into landscaped 'berms', heightening the sense of immersion for visitors as well as doing the practical task of sheltering the garden from the new car park. Paths loop around the garden, taking visitors more deeply into the planting and nestling the building into its woodland setting. Maggie's Southampton is a garden that links architecture, people and place. Continuity, seasonal change and well-being are key elements of this nurturing, recuperative space.

↓   At Maggie's Southampton, the corners of the building are clad in stainless steel to reflect the garden. Four blade walls are formed from rippling, earth-toned ceramic.

→   A sculptural, russet-barked Tibetan cherry (*Prunus serrula*) is an evolving focal point, used as an alternative to traditional sculpture.

↓   The painterly meadow-like planting palette is typical of Price's work. The choice of plants and their composition echo a wild space, inspired by the nearby New Forest.

←   A sense of immersion is key is to the success of the garden. Price was involved with the architects from the outset as is evident in the integration of the designs for building and garden.

↓   Paths flow around the building and the outdoor furniture is made from materials left over from the building's construction.

MALVERLEYS

Mat Reese,
Von Opel Family

NEWBURY, HAMPSHIRE
21st century
4 hectares / 10 acres

↓ The Terrace Garden borders flanking a narrow terrace are long and thin, and, to prevent the plantings from appearing linear, they are deliberately informal (self-seeders are encouraged). Specimens are allowed to flow over the hard surfacing, and variations in plant height are used to great effect.

Extensively developed and planted by head gardener Mat Reese since 2010, Malverleys is described by its owner, Emily von Opel, as an English flower garden, with its style drawing inspiration from eminent plantsmen's writings and their gardens, including Christopher Lloyd's Great Dixter (see page 120), William Robinson's Gravetye Manor (see page 128) and Vita Sackville-West's Sissinghurst Castle (see page 114).

A key consideration in the design process was to ensure that the garden created an elegant setting for the house while simultaneously melding with the surrounding countryside and taking advantage of the 'borrowed landscape' as part of a succession of prospects and vistas. Equally deliberate is the uniting trope of natural and uncontrived, the planting that is intentionally wilder and less manicured, while providing a successive palette of colour and seasonal delight. Deep mixed borders are the predominant form of planting, the planting schemes variously taking full advantage of annuals and bulbs, grasses and perennials, ferns, shrubs and trees. They are rich in form and texture, with scent used subtly but to good effect, and colour – of both flower and foliage – an important attribute.

Still, each of the fifteen generously sized garden rooms (the Cloister Garden, Cool Garden, East Border, Exotic Garden, Hot Garden, House Border, Parterre, Pond Garden, Stumpery, Terrace, Topiary Meadow, Walled Garden, Wedding Ring Border, White Garden and Woodland Walk) has a distinctive identity and personality bestowed by its specific planting, changes in level, and ornament, including garden buildings, sculpture, topiary and water features (fountains, pools and rills). A particularly enjoyable aspect of the layout are the narrow corridors between the yew hedges, which contrast with the more open spaces and allow the visitor to meander between the rooms. They make the garden a journey of discovery, surprise and delight, the sensory adventure heightened by the interplay of light and shade.

← Creating the interface between architecture and the wider gardens, the mixed House Border is the most intensively worked in the garden. The objective is year-round interest: carpets of tulips in spring, a jewel-like display in summer, mixing bedding and annuals, summer bulbs and perennials, as shown here. In colder seasons winter bulbs complement the form and colour of the shrubs.

↓ Enclosed by Cotswold stone walls and filled with the sound of water, the Cloister Garden is a tranquil lawned space. A central rill with its arching jets has strong echoes of the rill in the Generalife gardens in Spain; flanking it, rows of multi-stemmed *Prunus* 'Shirofugen' add a spring softness before giving a show of fiery leaf colour in autumn.

← The Cloister Garden in summer, when roses offer colour and scent. At the end of the rill is a tufa niche, occupied by a Coade stone sculpture of Neptune calming the waves, based on a famous work in the Louvre, Paris.

→ Seen across the Pond Garden, borders surrounding the pool and park beyond are reflected; the ornate chicken house is a distant eye-catcher.

↓ Enclosed by yew hedging and featuring four pools with fountains, the White Garden is restricted to tones of grey, green, silver and white. The foliage of *Cornus alternifolia* 'Argentea', *Eremurus* 'Joanna', *Gypsophila elegans* and *Orlaya grandiflora* is as important as their flowers.

↓ A summer view of the Topiary Meadow with its many yew forms, alongside the informality of the riot of wildflowers, creates a delightful contrast. The *Euonymus alatus* 'Compactus' hedge turns scarlet in autumn.

› [page 146] Within the Cool Garden, the four beds surrounding the central cauldron-like pool emphasize blue, mauve, purple and white flowers, complemented by blue-green, purple and silvery grey foliage and shrubs with fine, delicate leaves.

→ [page 147] The Stumpery, a modern take on a Victorian garden feature, is made from tree stumps positioned at theatrical angles. Mist irrigation enables the cultivation of ferns and adds drama to the woodland setting.

MALVERLEYS

HORATIO'S GARDEN

Cleve West

SALISBURY, WILTSHIRE
21st century
0.2 hectares / 0.5 acres

↓ Horatio's Garden is a therapeutic garden, a beautiful haven of several different areas, where soft, ephemeral planting creates a place of tranquility and rehabilitation for the patients of the Duke of Cornwall Spinal Treatment Centre and their families.

Horatio's Garden is a charity with the mission of bringing gardens to all National Health Service spinal-injury centres across England. The gardens are named after Horatio Chapple, who as a schoolboy volunteer observed that the Spinal Treatment Centre at Salisbury provided little outdoor space for patients and their loved ones. He initiated a project to rectify this but was tragically killed by a polar bear in 2011, aged just seventeen.

Appropriately, the first Horatio's Garden opened in Salisbury in 2012 and has the feeling of a sanctuary. Designer Cleve West ingeniously incorporated two stone walls shaped 'like spines, broken by an intersecting path before coming together in a continuous wall – a metaphor for every patient's recovery journey'. As well as providing seating, wheelchair-accessible paths, 2 metres (6 ½ feet) wide, of resin-bonded gravel, curve through mixed planting towards a large gathering space that draws the eye to the prospect of distant rolling hills. The planting – a mix of trees and shrubs, perennials, grasses and aromatic herbs – is carefully designed to be both aesthetically pleasing and stimulating to all senses through the combination of colour, form, scent, taste and texture. It is also intended to attract wildlife into the garden, and a rill that runs the length of an apple tunnel leading to a summerhouse brings the gentle babble of water.

The summerhouse is a place for quiet reflection or privacy, and a garden room provides a social space for patients and families, while the glasshouse and horticultural therapy area are used by patients for gardening activities or just to enjoy spending time outdoors; all these activities support patients' physical rehabilitation and psychological wellbeing. Even though the garden's specific design and purpose were to be therapeutic, West was surprised by the healing potential of gardens and horticulture: 'When I started, I didn't fully appreciate what Horatio's Garden was going to bring to people in terms of hope and sustenance and realigning their lives to cope with life-changing injuries.'

↑ A drystone wall in the shape of a spinal column provides seating, surrounded by red *Centranthus rubra* and the gently swaying *Stipa gigantea*.

↓ The peeling trunks of river willow (*Betula nigra*) are textural, while bear's breeches (*Acanthus mollis*) harmonize with regal lily (*Lilium regale*).

→ White plumes of *Aruncus dioicus* 'Horatio' nod to Horatio Chapple. This hybrid has bronze-tinted foliage that changes to coral and red in autumn.

IFORD MANOR

Harold Peto

BRADFORD-ON-AVON,
WILTSHIRE
20th, 21st century
1 hectare / 2.5 acres

Harold Ainsworth Peto was one of a group of British architects who found wealth designing country houses and gardens in the late nineteenth century. But Peto became disillusioned. In 1899 he moved into Iford Manor and lived there until his death in 1933.

Peto admired the terraced gardens of the Italian Renaissance, and the steep slope behind and to one side of his new home was ideal for the construction of terraces, augmented by pools and connected by steps. He used local stone, ornamenting the broad gravel walks on the terraces with original Italian statuary collected on his travels. He displayed more treasures in the courtyard that he called his Haunt of Ancient Peace.

The highest Great Terrace is colonnaded, with a stone seat at one end and an open-fronted *casita* at the other. In less skilled hands such a copyist approach might have been no more than *ersatz*, but Peto deftly re-created an Italian scene in the Wiltshire countryside. He combined the architectural frame with Arts and Crafts planting: cypress and juniper inject an Italian ambience, but Peto's use of hardy plants received approval from Gertrude Jekyll herself. In late spring the blooming *Wisteria sinensis* enhancing the flights of steps that link the terraces is particularly spectacular.

The garden is not entirely Italianate. Hidden in the woods above the terraces, where box (*Buxus sempervirens*) grows wild, is a small Japanese Garden. It may feel incongruous, but such gardens were all the rage at the turn of the twentieth century. To the east of the terraces, the garden takes on a medieval feel. A lawn in which *Lilium martagon* (the Turk's cap lily) has naturalized, echoing a flowery mead, leads to the Italian Cloister. To enter this airy structure is to enter another age. It is the perfect spot to reflect on Peto's masterful blurring of time and place. The present owners have restored the garden and its buildings, finishing the Oriental Garden and redesigning areas of the garden as they age.

↓ The colonnaded Great Terrace is lined with Harold Peto's classical statues.

↑ Near the Great Terrace some of Peto's original planting still survives, including box (*Buxus sempervirens*), which also grows wild in the woods above.

← Peto melded an Italian Renaissance-inspired framework of terraces with an Arts and Crafts planting scheme that softens its structure.

↓ The Italian Cloister is one of the largest buildings in the garden and today makes an atmospheric setting for concerts.

SHUTE HOUSE

Sir Geoffrey Jellicoe

DONHEAD ST MARY,
WILTSHIRE
20th century
0.8 hectares / 2 acres

Shute House is one of the finest gardens by one of the most influential twentieth-century landscape architects and garden designers, Geoffrey Jellicoe. It bears all the hallmarks of his design approach: structured geometry, vistas, water, human scale and respect for the *genius loci*. Trained as an architect, Jellicoe first worked at Shute House for Michael and Lady Anne Tree in the late 1960s, but the Water Garden for which the property is most famous dates from 1978. Even then the project was not complete, and Jellicoe was tempted out of retirement to finish the garden in what would be his last project when new owners arrived in 1994.

To the south of the house a grassy terrace terminates in a ha-ha, giving views over the borrowed landscape. To the west is a 'green bedroom', beyond which is a formal garden: a rectangle of six themed square beds of shrubs and flowers, each enclosed by box hedges. The Camellia Walk, with more than a hundred varieties, is spectacular in spring. At the

western perimeter is a romantic woodland garden, with statues and glades. Throughout the garden are carefully manipulated vistas.

Jellicoe's garden is really about water. A spring feeds the informal pools in the wood before becoming the River Nadder. The largest pool has a formal, rectangular arm, which Jellicoe modified to create the Canal Garden, enclosed with lofty hedges, headed by three herms and with twin grottoes. The famous Water Garden is set within a lawn but surrounded by dense plantings of perennials and trees that introduce a feeling of intimacy. A rill trips musically straight down the hillside over copper waterfalls into one square and two octagonal basins where gravity-fed, Kashmiri-inspired bubble fountains murmur. The composition has strong Islamic overtones and contrasts with the Western classical echoes elsewhere, but the Water Garden is nothing less than wholly modern in its execution and enchanting in its effect.

↓   The rill flows through square and octagonal pools with burbling bubble fountains towards a statue and a view of the landscape.

↖ Topiary creates the 'green bedroom' garden at the west side of the house.

↑ The rill tumbles over musical waterfalls whose pitch reflects the number of small copper V-shaped chutes that make up each one.

→ An arch supports a spectacular display of wisteria against a background of yew (*Taxus baccata*).

↓ The classically inspired Canal Garden is enclosed by tall beech hedges. Arum lilies (*Zantedeschia aethiopica*) thrive in the water.

SPILSBURY FARM

Tania and James Compton

TISBURY, NEAR SALISBURY,
WILTSHIRE
21st century
2.4 hectares / 6 acres

↓ The free-spirited garden at Spilsbury Farm is underpinned by strong structure, creating a space that is low-maintenance on a large scale.

Spilsbury Farm is the private garden of Tania Compton, garden designer and contributing Gardens Editor of *The World of Interiors*, and botanist James Compton, who for almost thirty years has been horticultural advisor at *Gardens Illustrated* magazine. The garden that spills out around their house is a reflection of Tania's free-thinking, free-spirited style, informed by James's eye for detail. This is essentially a low maintenance garden, but on a grand scale. It is deftly designed to be intentionally undermanaged.

At the front of the house is a gravel garden replete with lavender, perovskia and opportunistic self-seeders. From there, mown grass paths ribbon out through loose, shoulder-high meadow planting into a series of managed vistas. Deer-proof species roses with enough vigour to compete, such as the wild rose, *Rosa moyesii*, *R. rubiginosa* and *R. gallica* 'Versicolor', grow through the meadow to flower above the grasses during summer. There are copses of alder, liquidambar,

spindle and guelder rose, a nut walk underplanted with ferns, and an expansive pond with jetty, planted with native British species. Early in the year, spring bulbs introduce a 'gardened' element, with specialized species planted close to the house and broader drifts further afield.

The wildness of the garden is tempered by formality and underpinned by strong structure. Clipped cubes and tapering cones of topiary, and trees selected for their inherent good forms, such as *Carpinus* 'Globus' and 'Frans Fontaine', anchor the garden in its setting. Views are revealed and concealed over time.

James has turned the former tennis court into a place for horticultural research. The Comptons travel internationally on botanizing trips, and the old court is now a place to grow their wild collected plants. As part of his scientific research, James will visit and scrutinise a plant up to three times a day when he is studying it.

← Clipped cubes anchor an informal avenue of trees, underplanted with meadowsweet and creeping thistle.

↓ A loosely clipped *Buxus sempervirens* hedge, flanked by clouds of *Persicaria × fennica* 'Johanniswolke', leads to a grid of *Salix alba* var. *sericea* in the lower garden, near the former tennis court.

→ A jetty with a wooden seat overlooks the pond, offering expansive views beyond.

STOURHEAD

Henry Hoare II,
Henry Flitcroft

STOURTON, WILTSHIRE
18th century
40 hectares / 100 acres

↓ The classical architecture at Stourhead includes the decorative Turf Bridge across the lake, and the domed white Pantheon, based on the temple in Rome. The Grotto is visible on the far right.

In an age when most of the famous English landscapes were made by professional designers – William Kent, 'Capability' Brown and Humphry Repton – there were nonetheless a few notable gardens made by gifted amateurs. Arguably the finest is that at Stourhead, which Henry Hoare inherited from his banker father in 1724. On his return from his Grand Tour in 1741, Hoare began to create (with help from Henry Flitcroft) an Arcadian idyll with strong Claudian overtones. The project was funded by the interest paid on loans the Hoare bank was making to the landed gentry busy improving their own grand estates.

Hoare's Stourhead took almost thirty years to complete. A circuitous walk leads from the house anticlockwise around the lake, with strategically placed 'incidents' along the way. Carefully positioned, these incidents provide focal points and vistas and encourage movement along the route; more importantly, their form and type define the garden's programme: the journey of Aeneas

after he fled Troy but before he founded Rome. Aeneas would have recognized the classical temples, but the Grotto and the Pantheon – and perhaps also the Hermitage – might have flummoxed him, owing to their not-so-classical neighbours: the Chinese Bridge (now lost), the Turkish Tent, the Gothic Cottage, the Bristol High Cross, the Turf Bridge and the picturesque village of Stourton.

Today's visitor will notice another odd juxtaposition. One of the highlights of Stourhead is the nineteenth-century collection of trees and shrubs. These beautiful interlopers meld successfully with the classically inspired and naturalistic setting. They put on spectacular seasonal shows: rhododendrons in spring and fiery leaves in autumn. They grab the attention of horticulturists because many are unusual, and they add another layer of interest to the garden. But they are not authentic, a fact that raises a dilemma about whether Hoare's original garden should eventually be restored.

↑ A view through the arches of the stone Grotto reveals a statue of the River God.

↓ Rhododendrons flower beside the path around the lake.

← More rhododendrons cluster at the foot of the hill topped by the Temple of Apollo, dedicated to the sun god, which has fine views over the lake.

EAST LAMBROOK MANOR

Margery Fish

EAST LAMBROOK, SOUTH
PEVERTON, SOMERSET
20th century
0.5 hectares / 2 acres

After being widowed, Margery Fish poured her energy into her garden at East Lambrook, and in doing so reinvented the cottage garden for the twentieth century. Fish and her husband, Walter, had bought the house in 1937, a decade before his death. Rather than create compartments, borders and colour-coordinated planting, she took a naturalistic, informal approach, breaking with the prevailing Arts and Crafts tradition.

With a plantswoman's zeal and a designer's eye for arrangement, Fish developed a garden in which different areas flow seamlessly and are interesting all year. She used the various microclimates in the garden for those plants most suited to the specific levels of sun, moisture and so on. The garden was crammed with different plants, with no bare soil. The planting was so dense that it smothered most weeds, but if one appeared and looked good, Fish left it. The result was a weekend garden of great diversity yet requiring little maintenance.

Fish disseminated her ideas in various books, most notably *We Made a Garden*

(1956). Michael Pollan, reviewing a belated first US edition of 1996, called her 'the most congenial of garden writers, possessed of a modest and deceptively simple voice that manages to delicately layer memoir with horticultural how-to'.

Fish was passionate about perennials, and after World War II, when planting fashions began to shift towards shrubs, she recognized that many former favourites were in jeopardy. She set about collecting, propagating and, through her books, repopularizing them, and ensured their survival. Many of these perennials are in vogue again today, and a number are named after her garden, including *Artemisia absinthium* 'Lambrook Silver', *Euphorbia characias* subsp. *wulfenii* 'Lambrook Gold', *Santolina chamaecyparissus* 'Lambrook Silver' and *Primula* 'Lambrook Mauve'.

When Fish died in 1969 her garden went into decline, but successive new owners have restored it. Once again it is a beautiful and inspirational showcase of perennial planting at the highest level of the gardener's art.

↓ Snowdrops flower along a small stream; Fish favoured forms of hardy and adaptable native perennials.

↑   In the Cottage Garden, flowers include *Elaeagnus* 'Quicksilver', euphorbia, roses, phlomis, stachys and centaurea.

←   Moisture-loving plants flourish in The Ditch, including hellebores and *Scilla bithynica*.

↓   *Achillea*, *Thalictrum delavayi* and *Eschscholzia californica* in a border.

EAST LAMBROOK MANOR

HESTERCOMBE GARDENS

Coplestone Warre Bampfylde,
Gertrude Jekyll, Edwin Lutyens

CHEDDON FITZPAINE,
TAUNTON, SOMERSET
18th–20th century
20 hectares / 50 acres

↓ The formal walled Rotunda opens on to the terrace, which in turn gives on to the Great Plat below.

→ ↘ Figurehead fountains feed hemispherical pools that flow into rills along terraces on either side of the Great Plat. The rills are planted with various aquatic plants according to the varying depth of the water.

Hestercombe has two temporally and physically distinct gardens. The older – restored in the late twentieth century – is the picturesque landscape garden in the valley rising behind the house. Created by Coplestone Warre Bampfylde between 1750 and 1786, it has a circular path linking buildings and features, revealing contrived views. The path leads past the Pear Pond and up the valley, where the sound of falling water heralds the Great Cascade. At the top of the climb, the path passes through a dark laurel tunnel to spectacular vistas from the Gothic Alcove and the Capriccio View. The path zigzags down to the mausoleum and back to the Pear Pond, where, looking up, the full landscape is revealed and the Temple Arbour is reflected in the still waters. There is also a Victorian Shrubbery Garden, restored in 1999.

A gate in the wall leads to the formal garden, one of the finest results of the partnership of Gertrude Jekyll and Edwin Lutyens. The ingenuity of Lutyens, tightly controlled yet bold, asymmetrical geometry fits great beauty, variety and interest into a small space, while Jekyll provides a masterclass in planting.

Beyond the gate are the Dutch Garden and the Orangery, with its manicured lawn. Formal steps lead to the Rotunda, a water court that opens on to the terrace, below which lies the Great Plat, a sunken parterre divided diagonally by four grass paths edged with flagstones. In early summer the four beds are filled with bold groups of lilies, delphiniums and peonies, which give way to red cannas, gladioli and dahlias, reflecting the heat of mid- and late summer. Defining the end of the garden – and linking it with the borrowed landscape beyond – is the climber-clad pergola.

Above the Great Plat, in the East and West rills, water spouts from a fountain into a pool set into the wall. From each pool, water flows along a deep rill that runs the length of the lawn before splashing down steps into a water-lily tank. The rills are planted with water forget-me-not, iris and arum, and their straight lines are broken by whirlpools, which also help to control the flow.

HESTERCOMBE GARDENS

← [pages 162–163] A pergola designed by Lutyens forms the backdrop to the Great Plat.

↑ The classical Temple Arbour stands on top of a small wooded rise above the Pear Pond, which reflects it on a still day.

→ The path through the woodland leads past a hillside of foxgloves surrounding Pope's Urn, modelled on a design by William Kent for the poet Alexander Pope.

→ The Great Cascade in the Picturesque landscape garden crashes down a wooded cliff on to bare rock.

HESTERCOMBE GARDENS

HILLSIDE

Dan Pearson,
Huw Morgan

NEAR BATH, SOMERSET
21st century
0.2 hectares / 0.5 acre (garden);
8 hectares / 20 acres (wider landscape)

Hillside is the private garden of the garden designer Dan Pearson, overlooking a narrow valley near Bath in Somerset. It was originally a smallholding used most recently to raise beef cattle, but since moving there in 2010 Dan and his partner Huw Morgan have managed the land for increased biodiversity and native flora.

The 0.2 hectare (half-acre) ornamental perennial garden is part of 8 hectares (20 acres) of their land, parcelled by hedges into seven fields. Behind the stone house the land rises steeply to a lane, and in front it descends sharply to a glistening stream that runs through the woodland at the bottom of the valley. The perennial garden follows the line between the house and barn and is the most intensely worked part of the property.

Pearson is a world-leading garden designer who thinks like a plantsman. Hillside has a strong underlying layout – there are wide paths for free access and ease of movement when things are in full growth, and orderly steel-edged beds for practicality – but it is the plants and their combinations that are front and centre. At Hillside, swooping beds of beautiful textural, layered perennials and bulbs are completely at home in their rural setting. Plants such as eastern bluestar (*Amsonia tabernaemontana*) and *Baptisia* 'Twilite Prairieblues' jostle with tall, yellow-flowered *Thalictrum flavum* in high summer, stands of *Dierama pulcherrimum* overhang the path, and the tall grasses are speckled with sanguisorba – all part of an ongoing experiment in the creation of planting that echoes a wild place.

Further from the house, the land is less intensively worked. There is a vegetable patch, a new pond, an orchard and a nuttery of cobs and filberts, but otherwise it is predominantly pasture over-sown with local native wildflowers. The landscaping materials used at Hillside have been carefully considered and are in the rural vernacular. Bold architectural troughs, cast concrete steps, breeze block walls and corrugated iron clad buildings are the framework.

↓   At Hillside a south-facing perennial garden slopes down towards the fields and the 'Tump' beyond.

↑   In late summer, the view across the garden looking up towards the barn emphasizes the textural nature of the planting.

→   Granite troughs define the space, reflecting the sky and moon.

↓   Towering giant fennel (*Ferula communis*) offers a focal point in high summer.

167

THE NEWT

Margaret Hobhouse, Penelope Hobhouse,
Nori and Sandra Pope, Patrice Taravella

HADSPEN, NEAR BRUTON,
SOMERSET
19th, 20th, 21st century
12 hectares / 30 acres

The garden at Hadspen House has a long and illustrious pedigree, with various incarnations made by Margaret Hobhouse in the late nineteenth century, by Penelope Hobhouse in the 1960s and 70s, and by the Canadian couple Nori and Sandra Pope, who opened their innovative colour garden to the public in 1987 and remained there until the early 2000s. The latest manifestation, the brainchild of the South African couple Koos Bekker and Karen Roos, who purchased the estate in 2013, renamed it and converted the house into a hotel, is designed by Italo-French architect, chef and garden designer Patrice Taravella. (He created the gardens at Prieuré d'Orsan between 1991 and 2017.)

The key theme of Taravella's design, that a garden should be both beautiful and useful, dovetails neatly with evocations of different historic garden styles. The square beds of the Produce Garden, which grows more than 350 varieties of herbs, fruits and vegetables, many of which are used in the hotel kitchen, has overtones of a medieval monastery's productive garden. At the heart of the property, the egg-shaped former walled garden, now named the Parabola, features a Baroque-inspired multi-level maze planted with 267 apple tree cultivars, while the Long Walk has a Versailles-like *tapis vert* feel to its long, unbroken lawn. The Fragrance Gardens and Winter Gardens (conservatory) have Victorian origins, the latter celebrating the plant-hunters who introduced so many hothouse plants, in particular orchids from the world's tropics. In the Woodland Garden, qualities of the natural landscapes advocated by William Robinson are in evidence, and the area is also a diverse habitat for native wildlife. The Cottage Garden has echoes of Gertrude Jekyll's (see page 106) application of painterly colour theory to the planting, the Cascade is a contemporary twist on traditional water features, and the Colour Gardens nod their cheerful heads to the Popes' more recent manifestations at Hadspen.

In all, the garden exemplifies what a rich source of inspiration garden history may be, and how past ideas can be reinvigorated when creating a contemporary garden of elegance and refinement.

↓   The view across the formal Cascade Garden has an Islamic feel, with its geometric pools; the scene takes in the low hedge-edged beds of the juxtaposed Fragrant Victorian Garden. Below is the ebullient planting of the Colour Gardens, and beyond a prospect of the parkland.

← In the foreground is a display of Victorian bedding with sculptural castor oil plant (*Ricinus communis*) underplanted with red *Salvia* 'Ember's Wish' and *S. splendens* 'Go-Go Scarlet'. In the mid-ground, wall fountains gush into the pool of the Cascade Garden, and in the distance, behind the yew hedge, is the enclosed Cottage Garden.

↓ The Parabola is the new incarnation of the Walled Garden, formerly home to the spectacular colour garden created by Nori and Sandra Pope. Inspired by Baroque gardens, the layout is a series of intertwining maze-like circles constructed on various levels, retained by honey-coloured stone walls.

THE NEWT

← The Parabola features British apple cultivars arranged by county. Some form tunnels, and others are trained against the walls. The apples are used to produce estate cider.

→ The Red Garden – one of the gardens inspired by the work of Nori and Sandra Pope – is aflame in summer. *Crocosmia* 'Lucifer' dominates, with the ornamental grasses *Stipa gigantea* and *Nassella tenuissima* about to ignite.

↓ Below the Parabola, the Lower Egg is a serene lawn with mature trees, dotted with egg-shaped seating pods. The hornbeam hedge joins with the Parabola's walls to form an egg-shaped space of two contrasting halves. In the distance is the wildflower meadow, and beyond it the potager.

← Juxtaposed with the Victorian Garden and its bedding plants, but separated from it by a yew hedge, is the Gertrude Jekyll-inspired Cottage Garden. The cheerful, informal planting is artful and controlled, using many of Jekyll favourites, such as globe thistle, hollyhocks, lavender, bear's breeches (*Alchemilla mollis*), Mexican fleabane (*Erigeron karvinskianus*) and red bistort (*Bistorta amplexicaulis*).

OUDOLF FIELD, HAUSER & WIRTH SOMERSET

Piet Oudolf

BRUTON, SOMERSET
21st century
0.7 hectares / 1.5 acres

↓   The perennial garden at Hauser & Wirth Somerset plays permanent host to the Radić Pavilion, designed by Chilean architect Smiljan Radić, as well as various sculptures throughout the year.

→   Steel-edged ovals of grass punctuate the central path from the gallery through the 1.5 acre perennial meadow that is the Oudolf Field.

The Oudolf Field is a perennial garden by the landscape designer Piet Oudolf, an adjunct to Hauser & Wirth Somerset, an art gallery on the outskirts of Bruton. A perennial meadow – the Oudolf Field is laid out as seventeen beds of robust perennials and bulbs, with the Radić Pavilion at one end. Rudbeckia, echinacea, helenium, amsonia, actaea and veronicastrum are threaded through grasses including prairie dropseed (*Sporobolus heterolepis*) and *Deschampsia cespitosa* 'Goldtau'. Typical of Oudolf's style, the design celebrates plants at every stage in their life cycles, from shoot to flower to seed head, and emphasizes the plants' architecture post-bloom as much as their flower. What is important is 'the form of a flower and how it will last. I don't speak colour', says Oudolf.

The plants are arranged to benefit from the mercurial effects of light. Each plant is matched with appropriate space and company, and soil fertility is kept intentionally low so that the combinations balance and make a self-sustaining garden. Seed heads are left *in situ* throughout winter before every plant is pruned in spring, restarting a repeating cycle.

Visitors approach the Oudolf Field via the art gallery and the Cloister Garden, also designed by Oudolf. A shady space enclosed by walls and shade-loving plants, the latter is an atmospheric counterpoint to the main garden. A stylized take on woodland, it includes sculptural multi-stemmed paper mulberry trees, hakonechloa grasses and a choice selection of spring- and summer-flowering bulbs. The gallery owners regularly commission artists, and they took a similar approach when working with Oudolf, giving him a very open brief. The result is a breathtakingly beautiful and intensely seasonal garden.

← In the Cloister Garden, multi-stemmed paper mulberry trees (*Broussonetia papyrifera*) are underplanted with such shade-loving plants as *Euphorbia griffithii* 'Dixter', *Hakonechloa macra* and *Sesleria autumnalis* grass, and *Allium tripedale*.

↓ The long-lasting seed heads of *Echinacea pallida* are left *in situ* in late summer and autumn above bleached *Stipa tenuissima* grasses. Adjacent is *Helenium* 'Moerheim Beauty'.

→ [pages 174–175] Robust, textural perennials, including *Echinacea pallida* 'Hula Dancer', *Eryngium yuccifolium* and *Helenium* 'Moerheim Beauty', grow in midsummer with grasses, such as *Stipa tenuissima*.

DARTINGTON HALL

Leonard Elmhirst,
Dorothy Elmhirst, Henry Avray
Tipping, Beatrix Farrand, Percy Cane,
Preben Jacobsen, Dan Pearson

DARTINGTON, TOTNES,
DEVON
20th, 21st century
10 hectares / 25 acres

↓ ↘ The Tiltyard gives a view over the garden to the house. Leonard Elmhirst named it after a jousting arena, but in fact it was formerly the site of a pond. The clipped yews on the lawn terrace are known as the Twelve Apostles.

An ongoing mystery at Dartington Hall is who leaves flowers around the statue of Flora, the resting place of the ashes of Leonard and Dorothy Elmhirst, who transformed the property after they bought it in 1925. The statue also marks the transition from the Woodland Walk, designed by US landscape architect Beatrix Farrand, to the High Meadow, created by British designer Percy Cane.

The Elmhirsts (he was English, she American) took an experimental approach to their run-down estate. They rebuilt the fourteenth-century hall and made some bold new buildings. The gardens looked forwards rather than back. The first designer, Henry Avray Tipping, contributed in the Arts and Crafts style, adding hedges around the house to delineate 'rooms' and broadening the garden out into the valley.

Dorothy had worked with Beatrix Farrand in the United States, and she turned to her again; Farrand worked at Dartington from 1933 to 1938. She gave the Courtyard a collegiate atmosphere. Its wide paving, with bands of limestone setts and river cobbles, echoes her work on American university campuses. Her three Woodland Walks are also notable. She used 'backbone planting' to define areas with plant masses, and insisted on using natives, such as beech, holly and Scots pine. Cedars were added later, with *Magnolia grandiflora*, wisteria and camellias.

After 1945 Percy Cane accentuated the garden's external views and improved the Azalea Dell. He designed the Whispering Circle, the magnificent steps from the Glade to the Tiltyard, and the Heath Bank steps. Preben Jacobsen later designed a herbaceous border. Meanwhile, an impressive series of site-specific sculptures has been created for the gardens. Dan Pearson was commissioned in 2017 to reinvigorate the gardens and their relation to the surrounding landscape, making the estate as accessible and functional as possible and opening up vistas that had been lost to plant growth.

176

↑ → The Swan Fountain, created by Willi Soukop in 1950, stands on the steps designed by Percy Cane to link the garden with the woodland above.

↗ The Sunny Border in July has a fine show of nepeta, achillea, hemerocallis, agapanthus and echinops.

HOTEL ENDSLEIGH GARDENS

Humphry Repton

MILTON ABBOT, TAVISTOCK, DEVON
19th century
43.7 hectares / 108 acres

↓ The Grass Terrace overlooking the Tamar is now used for relaxed games of croquet.

→ [and page 180, top] Formal beds on the terrace near the hotel are filled with *Salvia viridis*; the rill on top of the stone wall is testament to Humphry Repton's fascination with moving water.

↘ The view over the Rose Walk and the Grass Terrace shows how Repton incorporated the formal elements near the house into the wider landscape.

If Lancelot Brown was 'Capability', the last of the great eighteenth-century landscape gardeners – Humphry Repton – would perhaps be best known as 'Practicality'. His designs combined beauty and convenience with comfort, privacy and social use. Hotel Endsleigh, overlooking the River Tamar in Devon, was built as a *cottage orné* by Jeffry Wyattville for the extravagant 6th Duke of Bedford. Repton's garden is from 1811 and was one of his favourite, and last, commissions. Shortly afterwards his carriage overturned and he sustained injuries that confined him to a wheelchair until his death in 1818.

The gardens, restored when the house was opened as a hotel in 2005, contain all Repton's signature features. Close to the house are formal gardens; beyond is the landscape. A grass terrace overlooks the Tamar, which the writer John Claudius Loudon described in 1842 as 'a clear and rapid river, passing through richly wooded banks', adding that he admired Endsleigh 'for its natural beauties,

and for the very high keeping displayed in all that we saw'. The arboretum contains trees from around the world, including ten 'Champion Trees', each the largest of its type in England.

Repton began his career in 1788, five years after the death of Brown, to whom he considered himself a worthy successor, although his approach was different. To create an appropriate transition between house and park, he made a terrace, often balustraded and ornamented with a covered veranda. On the terrace or juxtaposed with it, he placed a formal flower garden, screened from the park so that there was no jarring between artifice and nature. Repton's wooded and grassy landscapes were pierced by gravel drives and paths that followed the contours while keeping feet dry. He also used lakes with irregular outlines, and bays and promontories, rather than Brown's sinuous shapes, and he particularly enjoyed moving water in the form of rivers, streams and cascades.

HOTEL ENDSLEIGH GARDENS

↓   A circular fountain provides the focal point of the semicircular parterre.

→   The Rose Walk, roofed over with iron arches, is bordered by black-eyed Susan and geraniums.

HOTEL ENDSLEIGH GARDENS

PLAZ METAXU

Alasdair Forbes

TIVERTON, DEVON
20th–21st century
13 hectares / 32 acres

↓ Beyond the small garden behind the house, the pink berries of *Sorbus vilmorinii* show up well against *Fagus sylvatica* 'Dawyck' and *Quercus ilex* (holm oak).

→ Evergreen planting in the Hermes courtyard. A blacksmith's mandrel doubles as a magician's hat.

'Gardens of the mind' are rare today, but Alasdair Forbes's extraordinary garden landscape at Plaz Metaxu evokes the eighteenth century, not just in its spatial scope and concern with the classics, but also in its desire to express ideas and provoke thought. These ideas are not imposed, however – the garden can be enjoyed by anyone without engaging with any of its meaning.

The name Plaz Metaxu is Greek for 'the place between', expressing the idea of transition and a sense of tentative, searching space. A recurring theme in the garden is the transition from enclosed spaces to open vistas, in particular from parts of the landscape that are obviously gardened to those that look more like open countryside.

Many visitors to Plaz Metaxu experience a strong feeling of ambiguity. Much of the garden appears to mirror the surrounding Devon countryside, and yet everywhere there are reminders that this is not actually so: standing stones, inscriptions, stone circles, hedged enclosures that are difficult to imagine any countryman making, and patterns in stone that resemble pictures cut into chalk downs.

Although there are many views down the valley, to Forbes Plaz Metaxu is more a book than a picture: 'You can read a valley like the pages of a book. The stream along the bottom is like the binding. There is a unifying, cradling aspect to valleys, and the sides are always in dialogue with each other.'

Plaz Metaxu can be enjoyed simply as a mysterious space, but visitors are provided with a plan, along with a list of Greek deities and mythological figures to which different parts of the garden are dedicated (the old farmyard is devoted to Hermes; the front garden to Artemis, goddess of the moon). The design also reflects Eastern philosophies, such as Taoism, and the influence of numerous poets.

↑   This area is named Imbros after a site in ancient Greece. The stones represent man and boy.

↗   Spaces between parts of the garden are as important as the areas themselves.

↓   The old farm courtyard has been made into a sacred space, dedicated to Hermes, messenger of the gods.

→ Sunset over the valley shows the
close bond between garden and natural
landscape.

↓ On the Orexis mound, fillets of Delabole
slate draw the visitor's eye to the skies.

185　　　　　　　　　　　　　　　　　　　　　　PLAZ METAXU

SOUTH WOOD FARM Arne Maynard

BLACKDOWN HILLS,
DEVON
16th, 21st century
24.3 hectares / 60 acres

↓ The front of South Wood Farm faces east over a formal garden organized around an existing bay tree, now clipped into a dome. Intricate yew topiary is underplanted with low hedges of rosemary.

The success of the garden and landscaping at South Wood Farm lies in a sympathetic understanding of its ancient setting. Close to the house, designer Arne Maynard has created formal layouts within surrounding enclosures, but this formality gently melts into a wider landscape of orchards, a nuttery and swathes of long grass meadows speckled with wildflowers. When Professor Clive Potter bought the place, South Wood Farm sat in a crumbling jumble of barns and dereliction. But owner and designer shared a vision: a new setting that did not obliterate the texture of the old. Original walls, barns and outbuildings, now beautifully repaired, gather like comforting shawls around the thatched farmhouse.

A formal approach through tall stone pillars leads to the porch on the east front of the house. Handsome cubes of clipped yew contrast with old-fashioned borders of catmint and violas. A tall pleached screen of crab apple (a Maynard trademark) encloses the courtyard on the south side. Masses of old-fashioned roses – pink 'Cecile Brunner', mossy 'William Lobb' and cluster-flowered 'Bloomfield Abundance' – tumble over the stone walls.

These decorous enclosures close to the house, with their parterres and topiary, gently drift into wilder areas below and beyond the house. In 2019, Maynard returned to advise on a new pond, a modern remake of the old horse pond, with reed beds and a margin of wild iris. There are also plans to create an orchard of walnut trees, an ambitious extension of the nuttery that adjoins the kitchen garden to the north of the house.

The scheme that has evolved at South Wood Farm is entirely sympathetic to the vernacular buildings in this deeply rural setting, but it also includes occasional sharp and unexpected interventions, such as the clipped beech cones and pillars that serve as winter landmarks in the grassy area beyond the yard. The twenty-first century reaches back to the sixteenth to make a garden of intense delight.

→ An intricately cobbled path leads up from the farmyard to the strong geometry of the front garden, with its clipped yews and central bay tree.

↓ Attention to detail is the keynote of the garden, with native ferns encouraged to self-seed into the stone walls and paths.

↓ To the north of the farmhouse lies a magnificent kitchen garden, with raised beds edged in oak planks. Stepover apple trees guard crops of beans, peas, wallflowers and sweet williams, sown each year for the flower borders.

SOUTH WOOD FARM

WILDSIDE

Keith Wiley

NEAR BUCKLAND
MONACHORUM, DEVON
21st century
1.6 hectares / 4 acres

↓ On one of the upper slopes (the Canyons) at Wildside in midsummer are varieties of *Agapanthus* in slightly different shades of blue, complemented by the yellows of *Patrinia scabiosifolia*. Grasses play an important role later in the season.

Wildside is the perfect name for this innovative, idiosyncratic and very brave garden. Its sheer novelty is a powerful reminder of just how safe and unoriginal much garden-making is. Starting in 2004, Keith Wiley built on twenty years' experience working at a nearby garden, the Garden House. The climate in Devon is mild and wet, but the stone that Wiley dug into to create the network of hills and valleys that make up Wildside provides excellent drainage, so the possibilities for adventurous plant combinations are legion, especially in the Canyons, the most dramatic and recently developed part. Lower areas hit the water table, so valleys tend to be damp, with lush, moisture-loving plants.

Apart from one flat area, the Courtyard, this is a ruggedly sculpted terrain, perhaps comparable to an ambitious early twentieth-century rock garden or a Chinese scholar garden. There is the occasional view out, but this is essentially a garden that creates its own world. Slopes offer a wide range of micro-habitats, depending on their aspect, level of shade and moisture levels. These habitats are recognized and planted appropriately, which helps to push the plant diversity here into thousands of species.

Despite being very much in the spirit of contemporary naturalistic planting, the driving force here is artistic rather than ecological. Wiley has travelled widely and been inspired by a variety of semi-natural landscapes to create evocations of them here, along with others that arise purely from his own imagination. Much of the success of Wildside lies in recognizing what is doing well and giving those plants their head – so self-seeding of plants is encouraged and managed. The repetition of what Wiley calls 'foundation plants' helps to tie together what could be a very disparate whole. The remainder of the planting exploits all plant forms, from trees down to ankle-high creeping perennials, creating an artistic vision of vegetation that is rarely seen.

↑   A bridge over a pool in one of the lower, damper and older parts of Wildside. Astilbes thrive near the water's edge, while rodgersias and cultivars of *Crocosmia* in red and yellow grow among many other perennials on the banks.

↓   *Magnolia stellata* in spring, with blue *Muscari* 'Jenny Robinson', erythroniums and *Helleborus* × *hybridus* varieties. Later-flowering perennials often emerge here as these die back in the summer.

↑   *Agapanthus* 'Navy Blue' and 'Bressingham Blue' with yellow *Patrinia scabiosifolia* and *Stipa tenuissima*.

→   [pages 190–191]   The only level part of Wildside is a more formally designed area (the Courtyard), dominated by the striking forms of *Cordyline australis*. The tree-like shrub *Aralia elata* 'Variegata' is in the background, with *Agapanthus* cultivars in the foreground.

BARBARA HEPWORTH SCULPTURE GARDEN

Barbara
Hepworth

ST IVES, CORNWALL
20th century
0.1 hectares / 0.2 acres

↓ ↘ →   Barbara Hepworth's garden of different levels, steps and profuse planting creates an outdoor gallery for her stone or bronze sculptures in which the natural shapes of the plants both echo and contrast with the smooth yet organic forms of the works of art. The pieces on display include Hepworth's *Corymb* (below, left), *Sphere with Inner Form* (opposite, front) and *Four Square* (*Walk Through*) (opposite, back).

The British sculptor Barbara Hepworth conceived her Cornish garden as a creative space in which she could think, as well as to display her increasingly large works. She made a sculpture and then placed it where it would best fit into the garden, rather than producing pieces for particular locations. The result is an outdoor gallery that expresses the essence of her approach to her work.

Hepworth moved to Cornwall at the outbreak of World War II, in 1939, with her husband, the artist Ben Nicholson, and their young family. A decade later they bought Trewyn Studio, a typical St Ives stone-built house with what Hepworth described as 'a studio, a yard and garden where I could work in open air and space'. She lived and worked there until her death in 1975, when she was killed in a fire that gutted the studio. Hepworth's will required that the studios and garden be opened to the public; the property has been managed by Tate since 1980.

When she designed the walled garden in the early 1950s, Hepworth was in the process of establishing herself as one of Britain's leading abstract sculptors. She was experimenting with large-scale bronze works well suited to outdoor display, and the garden would be a vital viewing area for these large works.

With her friend the composer Priaulx Rainier, Hepworth laid out a garden that works its way down the sloping site in a series of paths and flower beds. Many of the beds feature sculptural, evergreen plants in shades of green. Bamboo, cordyline, phormium and Chusan palm (*Trachycarpus fortunei*) give the garden a subtropical feel while simultaneously creating a stage on which the sculptures are the stars. The shadows cast by the trees add dynamism and volume to the works, which in turn provide a still framework and visual punctuation to the naturalistic planting.

The topography, planting and artworks unite in a harmonious but varied whole that offers a unique insight into how the artist perceived and developed the relationship between her abstract, motionless sculptures and the dynamic, organic garden.

BARBARA HEPWORTH SCULPTURE GARDEN

THE LOST GARDENS OF HELIGAN

Tremayne Family

PENTEWAN, ST AUSTELL,
CORNWALL
19th–20th century
32.4 hectares / 80 acres

↓ Restored in 1996, the Sundial Garden was the location of what *Gardener's Chronicle* in 1896 called the finest herbaceous border in England.

Set on the south Cornish coast, Heligan was one of the many large country-house gardens for which World War I sounded the death knell. Such gardens relied on ample labour, cheap fuel to warm the glasshouses, and low taxes – all of which were absent after the conflict. Heligan was abandoned until the 1990s, when it was rediscovered, renamed – the 'Lost Gardens' – and restored.

The garden structure is eclectic. As with other gardens on the Cornish coast, the house stands at the head of a sheltered valley that here runs down to the fishing village of Mevagissey. Now named 'The Jungle', this part of the garden was developed in the late nineteenth century and boasted a collection of hardy and slightly tender perennials, shrubs and trees from all over the world, which thrived in the valley's microclimate. The surviving specimens are now mature, but the replanting aesthetic has been to maintain the romantic 'jungle' feel of the overgrown garden rather than restore the structured planting.

Unusually, the Northern Gardens lie behind and completely separate from the house. There are also two walled gardens with glasshouses and a famous pineapple pit, as well as a large 'open ground'. These are gardened organically and planted with heritage or heirloom varieties.

Surrounding the productive gardens are various ornamental areas: the Sundial Garden, with its herbaceous border and handkerchief tree (*Davidia involucrata*); Sikkim, with its collection of rhododendrons; the enclosed Italian Garden, with its pool; and the Ravine, with its rocky outcrops. Floras Green is a large lawn surrounded by rhododendrons with a perimeter walk that takes in views of the garden and offers vistas over rolling countryside to the sea.

↑ *The Mudmaid* was created by local artists Sue and Pete Hill as a version of Victorian garden 'ornamentation'.

→ A statue of *Pluto with a Dolphin* stands in the pond in the Italian Garden. Previously known as the Suntrap, this was the first garden at Heligan to be restored.

↓ The productive gardens grow over 200 old-fashioned varieties of fruit and vegetable using similar methods to those employed by the Victorian gardeners at Heligan.

→ [pages 196–197] Rhododendrons flower amid tree ferns (*Dicksonia antarctica*) and other exotics (including Chusan palms, *Trachycarpus fortunei*) in the Jungle, thanks to the microclimate of the steep-sided valley.

THE LOST GARDENS OF HELIGAN

TRESCO ABBEY GARDENS

Augustus Smith,
Dorrien-Smith Family

TRESCO, ISLES OF SCILLY
19th–20th century
7 hectares / 17 acres

On the private island of Tresco in the Isles of Scilly, five generations of dedicated garden-makers have used the warming effect of the Gulf Stream to create a remarkable garden on three terraces. The Lighthouse Walk and Neptune Steps provide vertical access between, and paths wind up and down the sloping site amid richly planted beds filled with exotic varieties.

Tresco's more than 20,000 exotic plants thrive in the Mediterranean climate. They come from more than eighty countries, as reflected in such named areas as Mexico, South Africa Cliff, and both Higher and Lower Australia. Within the garden, microclimates suit plants from specific regions. The shade at the foot of the terraces, for example, suits New Zealand and South American plants, such as *Cyathea* tree ferns and Norfolk Island pine (*Araucaria heterophylla*). The partly protected middle terrace nurtures plants from the Canary Islands and South Africa (including passion flowers) and agave and puya from South America. The sunny top terrace is home to plants from dry regions of

Australia and South Africa, such as banksia, protea, aloe and Cape heaths.

The banker Augustus Smith began to make the garden in 1834 around the ruins of a twelfth-century priory. An avid plant-collector, he soon ran out of space and created the steep, south-facing terraces the garden occupies today. In 1872 Tresco passed to his nephew Thomas Algernon Dorrien-Smith, who planted extensive shelter belts of trees on the garden perimeter in order to protect the plants from winter gales. The next owner, Major Arthur Dorrien-Smith, added to the collection, not least with plants from collecting trips to New Zealand and the Chatham Islands. From 1955 Commander Tom Dorrien-Smith focused his collecting activities on plants from South Africa and Australia, in particular the family Proteaceae. Under the current owners, Robert and Lucy Dorrien-Smith, much restoration was required after hurricanes in 1987 and 1990, but the garden continues to develop and to justify its worldwide reputation.

↓   Mixed planting on the Middle Terrace includes agave, cordyline, echium, *Geranium maderense* and palms.

↑ A young Canary Island palm (*Phoenix canariensis*) grows next to an arch from the twelfth-century Benedictine priory.

← The dry and sunny Upper Terrace is home to succulents and proteas, most of which originate mainly in Australasia and South Africa.

↓ The statue of 'Neptune' at the top of the Neptune Steps is in fact a figurehead salvaged from the Steamship SS *Thames*.

↑ The rays of the early-morning sun illuminate the Shell House in the Mediterranean Garden.

↓ The Middle Terrace is sheltered, and thus suitable for plants from a range of climate zones.

↑→ Drought-tolerant plantings of herbaceous species and succulents include a bank of *Lampranthus spectabilis* 'Tresco Fire', *Amaryllis belladonna* and *Aeonium arboreum* 'Atropurpureum'.

TRESCO ABBEY GARDENS

Glossary

Allée
A formal, straight walk or path that is bordered by trees or by clipped hedges.

Annuals
In gardens, annuals are usually brightly coloured flowers that go through their entire life cycle in a year: their seeds are sown in spring, they are planted out to flower in summer, and they die in the autumn. Tender annuals are often used for bedding.

Arabesque
An ornamental design of intertwined, flowing lines, sometimes used in parterres.

Arboretum
An ornamental collection of trees and shrubs that often has botanical value, as a display of native or introduced species.

Architectural Plant
A term that refers to large, woody perennial or evergreen plants – often with a distinctive form or shape – that give structure or definition in a garden.

Arts and Crafts
A garden style perfected by the work of Gertrude Jekyll and Edwin Lutyens in the first decades of the twentieth century, using garden 'rooms' and close integration of built structures. Arts and Crafts was the dominant approach in garden design throughout much of the twentieth century.

Baroque
A highly ornate style of art and architecture popular in seventeenth- and eighteenth-century Europe; Baroque gardens are formal, and include features such as richly carved fountains, grottoes and elaborate statuary.

Bedding
Planting out dense arrangement of bulbs in spring and tender annuals in summer in order to create massed patterns of colour. A very labour-intensive method of gardening, popular in Victorian times.

Belvedere
A pavilion or other purely decorative structure built on a raised area as a viewpoint over the surroundings.

Botanic
A botanic garden is dedicated to the collection and display of a wide range of plants with their botanical names, often with specialist groupings.

Borrowed Landscape
The landscape beyond a garden when it is deliberately included in the garden design, such as by the use of views and vistas and the ha-ha.

Bosquet
A group of trees planted to form a decorative glade enclosed by a hedge or fence, often as part of a seventeenth- or eighteenth-century French formal landscape garden.

Border
A strip of ground at the edge of a garden or walk used for ornamental planting.

Bulbs
A general word for plants that grow from an underground source, such as a corm, tuber or rhizome.

Canopy
A layer of foliage created by the leaves of trees.

Cascade
A word for any dramatic fall of water.

Chahar Bagh
A Persian or Turkic term that means 'four-part garden'; it commonly describes a walled Islamic garden divided into four parts by water channels. This quadripartite layout is found throughout the Muslim world.

Chinoiserie
A quasi-Chinese style of decoration adopted by European designers in the seventeenth and eighteenth centuries, based more on travellers' descriptions of East Asia than on any familiarity with Chinese models.

Conservatory
A greenhouse in which plants are displayed.

Cottage Garden
An informal garden usually planted with a mixture of flowering plants and edible crops.

Cultivar
A variety of plant that has been created artificially through cultivation and breeding.

Dry Garden
A garden based on plants that require little, if any, watering beyond natural rainfall, often utilising aggregate surfacing to minimise evaporation from the soil.

English Landscape Style
A style of large-scale naturalistic garden design that began on English country estates in the early eighteenth century, when gardens were designed with complex symbolic or political messages, expressed as buildings and landscape features. A purely visual version – setting out to evoke an idealized pastoral landscape – spread throughout Europe in the eighteenth and nineteenth centuries.

Espalier
To train a fruit tree or ornamental shrub to grow flat against a wall, usually to take advantage of the sun and to make the fruit easy to pick.

Eye-Catcher
A feature such as a tower or a 'ruin' deliberately placed in the landscape to create a focal point for a broad vista.

Event
A term that refers to the central focus of an area of a garden, such as a viewpoint, a particular arrangement of plants, a sculpture, a water feature or any combination of such elements.

Exotics
Plants that do not occur naturally in a particular region. They may be hardy or tender.

Folly
A building or other structure intended to be decorative rather than useful; follies often resemble historic, ruined or fantastical structures.

Gazebo
A small roofed building, sometimes with open sides, usually offering extensive views.

Gravel Garden
A garden in which a layer of gravel is spread over the ground; gravel gardens suit low-maintenance, drought-tolerant plants.

Groundcover
Low-growing, spreading plants that are used partly to stop weeds growing.

Ha-ha
A dry ditch with a vertical wall on one side, used as a sunken 'fence' to keep livestock out of landscape gardens without interrupting the view with a visible barrier.

Herbaceous Border
A border planted mainly with perennials.

Herbarium
A collection of dried plants arranged to be studied.

Hortus Conclusus
Latin for 'enclosed garden', the term describes an enclosed medieval garden with low hedges, flowers and herbs.

Islamic Garden
A garden based on traditional Islamic styles, in which gardens were walled reminders of paradise, with quadripartite layouts, ample use of water, and a planting of symbolic flowers and trees.

Italianate
A nineteenth-century garden style popularized by Sir Charles Barry that amalgamated Italian, French, British, and Dutch Renaissance and Baroque ideas and features.

Knot Garden
A type of enclosed garden originating in sixteenth-century Tudor England, in which an

intricate and symmetrical pattern is created by low evergreen hedges – often box, yew or thyme – sometimes filled in with brightly coloured flowers or gravel.

Meadow Style
A nature-inspired garden planted with wildlife-friendly and native grasses, annuals and perennials.

Mediterranean Garden
A style of garden that evolved in Mediterranean climates, planted primarily with plants that grow in a similar climate all over the world.

Modernism
A functional, minimalist architectural style that originated in the 1920s, often using modern materials such as concrete. In garden design, Modernism took a similar approach, often using simple shapes, flat textures and limited blocks of colour.

Mughal Garden
A style of garden associated with the Islamic Mughal dynasties that ruled northern India, Pakistan and Afghanistan from the sixteenth to nineteenth centuries. Mughal gardens were based on the Islamic tradition, with symmetrical, axial layouts, quadripartite *chahar bagh*, stone terracing, water chutes and channels, and open-air pavilions.

Natives / Native Plants
Plants that naturally occur in the wild in a particular area.

Naturalistic Planting
An informal planting style in which hardy plants – herbaceous perennials, shrubs, trees and bulbs, both native and introduced – are arranged in beds and borders to best display their individual and collective attributes and beauty. Naturalistic planting was first popularised in the late nineteenth century by the Irish plantsman and writer, William Robinson.

Naturalize
To introduce a non-native plant so that it grows wild in a particular area.

New Perennial Movement
A gardening movement originating in northwestern Europe and the Prairie Movement in the USA in the 1970s and 1980s, that evolved from an approach pioneered in Germany in the 1930s. It emphasized mass plantings of perennials and ornamental grasses and retained seed heads and dead grasses as an autumn and winter display.

Orangery
A stone or heated structure with large windows that is used for growing oranges and other tender ornamentals.

Ornamental Grasses
Annual or perennial grasses that are grown for their colour or texture.

Palissade
A clipped hedge, often hornbeam, that forms a green wall along an allée.

Parterre
An ornamental flower garden in which the beds and paths are arranged to create a pattern.

Parterre de Broderie
French for 'embroidered parterre', this term refers to particularly intricate flowing designs made of box against a background of grass, gravel or turf and planted with colourful flowers. Commonly used in Baroque gardens.

Pavilion
A light, roofed structure that can be ornamental and that is often used for entertaining.

Perennials
Plants that die back to an underground root every year after flowering; they regrow the following spring.

Picturesque
An eighteenth-century English landscape style based on an artistic and literary movement that celebrated the power of untamed nature.

Pinetum
A collection of conifers.

Pleach
To entwine or interlace the branches of trees to form a hedge or provide continuous cover.

Potager
A type of decorative kitchen garden that emerged in formal French gardens in the seventeenth and eighteenth centuries; potagers use box or other hedging to define beds and often contain vegetables grown partly for their appearance, such as the famed purple cabbages of Villandry in France.

Prairie Garden Movement
The first truly native inspired American garden style. It emerged in the late nineteenth century in and around Chicago, and drew inspiration for design and planting from the natural landscape and flora of the mid-West.

Renaissance
The revival of European art and literature under the influence of classical models in the fourteenth to sixteenth centuries.

Rill
A narrow, shallow artificial stream or rivulet running between areas of a garden; rills can be either straight – as in the Persian gardens where they originated – or serpentine. They are usually lined with stone.

Rock Garden
A garden that is laid out among a naturally or artificially rocky area with spaces for plants such as alpines.

Serpentine Paths
Curving paths running through areas of shrub and tree planting or meadows.

Shrub
A small plant with a number of woody stems that separate at or just above ground level.

Succulent
A drought-tolerant plant with thick, fleshy leaves or stems that it uses to store water.

Tapis Vert
French for 'green carpet', used to describe a close-cropped expanse of grass, especially as part of a formal scheme.

Terminus
A feature – such as a building, rock or specific plant – that is placed at the end of a vista.

Terrace
An external, raised, open and flat area, usually on the side of a hill or slope.

Topiary
The art of clipping evergreen plants, such as box and yew, into abstract or figurative shapes.

Trompe-l'Oeil
From the French for 'deceive the eye', an effect designed to alter normal perception, often used in gardens to increase distances and change perspectives. It can take the form of out-of-scale plantings, trellises, mirrors or painted surfaces.

View
An attractive prospect across a natural or designed landscape.

Vista
A long, narrow view that is often defined by trees or buildings.

Water Feature
Any kind of pond, fountain or rill used in a garden.

Water Garden
A garden, or part of a garden, the main purpose of which is to grow and display water plants in pools, canals or streams.

Wilderness
An enclosed but informal area in a landscape garden, planted with trees and shrubs.

Winter Garden
An alpine or rock garden, or an indoor heated conservatory for the display of exotic plants.

Further Reading

The Garden Book, Revised and Updated Edition (Phaidon Press, 2021)

The Gardener's Garden (Phaidon Press, 2014, 2017)

Baker, Barbara, *Dream Gardens of England: 100 Inspirational Gardens* (Merrell Publishers, 2010)

Bisgrove, Richard, *The National Trust Book of the English Garden* (Viking, 1990)

Bradley-Hole, Kathryn, *English Gardens: From the Archives of Country Life Magazine* (Rizzoli International, 2019)

Buchan, Ursula, *The English Garden* (Frances Lincoln, 2006)

Campbell, Katie, *Icons of Twentieth-Century Landscape Design* (Frances Lincoln, 2006)

Compton, Tania, *The Private Gardens of England* (Constable, 2015)

Edwards, Ambra, *The Story of the English Garden* (HarperCollins Publishers, 2018)

Hobhouse, Penelope, *The Story of Gardening* (Dorling Kindersley Publishers Ltd, 2002)

Jellicoe, Geoffrey, Susan Jellicoe, Patrick Goode and Michael Lancaster, *The Oxford Companion to Gardens* (Oxford University Press, 2001)

Musgrave, Toby, *The Head Gardeners: Forgotton Heroes of Horticulture* (Aurum Press, 2009)

Musgrave, Toby, *The Garden: Elements and Styles* (Phaidon Press, 2020, 2023)

Quest-Ritson, Charles, *The English Garden: A Social History* (Penguin Books Ltd, 2001)

Richardson, Tim, *The New English Garden* (Frances Lincoln, 2013)

Spencer-Jones, Rae, *1001 Gardens You Must See Before You Die* (Cassell Illustrated, 2007)

Wilson, Andrew, *Influential Gardeners: The designers who shaped 20th-century garden style* (Mitchell Beazley, 2005)

Directory

This directory provides a list of gardens open to the public and featured in this book – gardens that can be visited throughout the year, or by prior arrangement, or on regular open days. Please check individual garden websites for opening hours and visiting information. Many of the gardens illustrated are private and not open to the public, or they offer restricted visitor access through organizations such as the National Garden Scheme. Any garden not listed in the directory can be assumed to fall into this category.

Cornwall
The Lost Gardens of Heligan, Pentewan, St Austell
Barbara Hepworth Sculpture Garden, St Ives

Cumbria
Levens Hall, Kendal
Rydal Hall, Rydal
Lowther Castle & Gardens, Penrith

Buckinghamshire
Stowe

Derbyshire
Chatsworth, Bakewell

Devon
Wildside, Near Buckland Monachorum
Dartington Hall, Dartington, Totnes

East Sussex
Great Dixter, Northiam, Rye

Essex
The Beth Chatto Gardens, Elmstead Market
Harlow Town Park Water Garden, Harlow
The Gibberd Garden, Harlow

Gloucestershire
Hidcote Manor, Hidcote, Bartrim
Sezincote, Moreton-in-Marsh

Hampshire
Exbury Gardens, Exbury, Southampton

Herefordshire
The Laskett Gardens, Much Birch

Hertfordshire
Hatfield House, Hatfield

Isles of Scilly
Tresco Abbey Gardens, Tresco

Kent
Sissinghurst Castle Garden, Sissinghurst, Near Cranbrook
Prospect Cottage, Dungeness

Lancaster
Gresgarth Hall Gardens, Caton

London
Barbican Conservatory and Gardens
Hands off Mangrove Garden
The Royal Botanic Gardens, Kew

Norfolk
East Ruston Old Vicarage Garden, East Ruston, Norwich
The Bressingham Gardens, Bressingham

Northamptonshire
Cottesbrooke Hall, Northampton

Northumberland
Alnwick Garden, Alnwick

Oxfordshire
Rousham House, Steeple Aston
Blenheim Palace, Woodstock

Staffordshire
Biddulph Grange, Biddulph, Stoke-on-Trent
Trentham Gardens, Stoke-on-Trent

Somerset
Oudolf Field, Hauser & Wirth, Bruton
The Newt, Hadspen, Near Bruton
East Lambrook Manor, East Lambrook, South Peverton
Hestercombe Gardens, Cheddon Fitzpaine, Taunton

Surrey
Hampton Court Palace, East Molesey

Warwickshire
Kenilworth Castle & Gardens, Kenilworth

West Sussex
Denmans, Fontwell, Arundel
Gravetye Manor, East Grinstead

Wiltshire
Stourhead, Stourton
Iford Manor, Bradford-on-Avon

Index

Page numbers in *italics*
refer to illustrations

Acknowledgements

We are particularly indebted to consultant editor Toby Musgrave and garden designer Tania Compton for their vital contributions to this book and for writing the foreword and introduction. We would also like to thank Annie Guilfoyle, Anna Pavord and Juliet Roberts for their knowledge, passion and sound judgement.

We are grateful to the following contributors for their texts:

Lucy Bellamy (pp. 16, 100, 110, 134, 138, 140, 154, 166, 172); Katie Campbell (pp. 78, 120); Ruth Chivers (pp. 12, 58, 74, 124, 176); Tim Cooke (p. 112); Noel Kingsbury (pp. 182, 188); Anna Pavord (p.186); Toby Musgrave (pp. 10, 14, 18, 20, 24, 30, 34, 44, 46, 48, 50, 62, 64, 66, 70, 80, 88, 90, 92, 96, 102, 104, 106, 114, 128, 136, 142, 148, 150, 152, 156, 158, 160, 168, 178, 192, 194, 198); Jill Raggett (pp.54, 84); Barbara Segal (p.40) and Chris Woods (p.36).

Additional thanks are due to all the garden owners, designers and gardeners who gave us permission to include their gardens.

Editorial Note

The gardens in this book are arranged geographically, by county, running from north to south. The order of gardens within each region is arranged alphabetically by name. Garden sizes are provided when known. Some gardens change over time, however, and sources sometimes vary or accurate figures may be unavailable. In such cases, we have used the most commonly accepted figure.

Picture Credits

Courtesy Aga Khan Centre: Photograph © John Sturrock 92, 93t, 93b; © Allan Pollock-Morris: 20, 22, 23tl, 23b; Courtesy Allen Scott Landscape Architects: 90–1; Andrea Jones/Garden Exposures Photo Library: 19tl, 19tr, 43, 79m, 102, 124, 125, 126, 152, 153m, 160, 179b, 195b, 199bl; Andrew Findlay/age Fotostock: 19m; © Andrew Montgomery: 120, 121t; © Andrew Lawson: 21br, 21t, 21bl, 23tr, Serge Hill Barn/designer Tom Stuart-Smith 78, 79tz, Hampton Court Palace 105t, Designer Alasdair Forbes 184tl, 184tr, 185b, Prospect Cottage/Design the late Derek Jarman 113tl, 113bl, 113br; Arcaid Images/Alamy: 74, 75br; Barbara Opitz Bildarchiv Monheim: 161b; © Bastin et Evrard: 151b; © Bowness, Hepworth Estate/Photo © Tate Images: 192l; Carole Drake/Alamy: 13tr, 13b; Caroline Jones/Latitude Stock Images/age Fotostock: 59t; Courtesy Chatsworth: 24; © Claire Takacs: 17t, 79b, 96–8, 129br, 129bl, 130–31, 132, 133t, 142, 143t, 144, 145–7, 188–91; © Clive Nichols: 28b, 35t, 35m, 47br, 64–5, 75bl, 76, 127b, 148–49, 168, 169b, 171t, 199br, 200tl; © Country Life: 61br; Corbis/Peter Barritt: 193; Craig Roberts/Photolibrary/Getty Images: 13m; 18–19; David Pearson/Alamy: 176; Photography by Eva Nemeth: 166–67; Florian Monheim/Bildarchiv Monhim GmbH: 105b, 104; foto-zone/Alamy: 49bl; Gap Photos: A. Butler 54, 55t, 55b, 57b, Andrew Lawson 56, 57t, Carol Casselden 121br, Carole Drake 67b, Charles Hawes 25t, 25b, 46, 69b, 164t, 177, Clive Nichols 13tl, Dianna Jazwinski 158, John Glover-Design Gertrude Jekyll 107b, 108–9, Jonathan Buckley 85, 122–23, Marcus Harpur 87t, Matt Anker 59br, Matteo Carassale 11tr, 11tl, Richard Bloom 36–9, 79tl, Rob Whitworth 35b; The Garden Collection: Andrew Lawson 48, 49tl, 49br, 49tr, 63tl, 88, 127t, 153tr, 153b, 153tl, 164b, 165, Andrew Lawson/Prospect Cottage/Designer the late Derek Jarman 113tr, Clay Perry 161t, Derek Harris 103b, 107t, 151tl, 196–97, 198, Jacqui Hurst 41b, 192r, Jerry Harpur/Hatfield House, Hertfordshire 81t, 81br, 81bl, John Glover 103tr, 121bl, 159bl, Modeste Herwig 31tr, 314, © Neil Sutherland/ Designer the late Derek Jarman 112, Nicola Stocken Tomkins 41t, 75t; Courtesy Gravetye Manor. Photo: Paul Johnson: 129t, 128; Courtesy Grow2Know/Neil Marshment Photography: 100r; Courtesy Hotel Endsleigh: 178; © Harpur Garden Images/Corbis: 82–3, 150; © Hugh Palmer: 31m, 63tr, 69tl, 69tr; Photograph Huw Morgan: 28t; Courtesy Iford Manor: 151tr; © Jason Ingram: 26–7, 29t, 47t, 47bl, 100l, 101, 111br, 143b, 169b, 170, 171m, 171b, 172–75, 186–87; Jerry Harpur/Harpur Garden Images: 11br, 12, 40, 44, 45b, 45tl, 45tr, 87m, 201, 200tr; Jerry Harpur/Hatfield House, Hertfordshire/Harpur Garden Images: 80; © John Sturrock, Courtesy KXCLP: 94–5; Julian Stephens/Heligan Gardens Ltd.: 195t; Courtesy Kim Wilkie and Pip Morrison: 138–39; © Liz Every/Garden World Images:58, 59bl; Lorna Tremayne/Heligan Gardens Ltd.: 195m; Courtesy Maggie's Centre/ © Hufton+Crow: 140, 141tr; Marcus Harpur/Harpur Garden Images: 42, 66, 68, 84, 86, 87b, 116b, 136, 137t, 137br, 137bl, 159t, 159br; Marcus Harpur/Harpur Garden Images/Designed by Gertrude Jekyll: 106; Marianne Majerus/MMGI: 89t, 89m, 89b, 133b, 179t, 180t, 180b, 181; Matt Gibson/age Fotostock: 103tl; © National Trust Images: Andrew Butler 30, 70, 71m, 71b, 72–3, Andrew Lawson 51, 52, 53t, David Dixon 115, David Sellman 53b, Derek Harris 157tr, James Dobson 156, Jason Ingram 118–19, Jerry Harpur 71tl, Jonathan Buckley 53m, 116t, 117t, 117bl, 117br, McCoy Wynne 31b, Nick Meers 31tl, Oliver Benn 32–3, Rupert Truman 71tr, Simon Knight 157tl, Stephen Robson 50, Timothy Smith 157b; Ngoc Minh Ngo: 16, 17br, 17bl; Olaf Protze/age Fotostock: 62–3; © RHS/Neil Hepworth: 182, 183, 184b, 185t; © Richard Bloom: 14–15, 29b, 110, 111t, 111bl, 134–35, 154–55; Robin Stott/www.geograph.co.uk: 67t; Photograph by Sarah Price: 141tl, 141bl, 141br; Shutterstock/cktravels.com: 99; © Skyscan Photolibrary/Alamy: 63m; © Toby Musgrave: 114, 194, 199t, 200b; Upton Wold – by kind permission of Mr and Mrs Ian Bond, photograph by Mary Best: 60, 61t, 61bl.

Phaidon Press Limited
2 Cooperage Yard
London E15 2QR

Phaidon Press Inc
65 Bleecker Street
New York
NY 10012

phaidon.com

This edition (published in 2023) is an abridged, revised, and updated version of *The Gardener's Garden* (first published in 2014)
© 2014, 2023 Phaidon Press Limited

ISBN 978 1 83866 634 7

A CIP catalogue record for this book is available from the British Library and the Library of Congress.

Commissioning Editor: Victoria Clarke
Editorial Assistant: Caitlin Arnell Argles
Production: Gif Jittiwutikarn
Design: Lacasta Design

Printed in China